called to influence

A New Approach to Life, Education
and College Admissions

what others have to say

"It's a true blessing to have a roadmap for my sons' education. I appreciate being able to learn from someone who has already blazed the homeschool trail to college. The plan (we developed together) even highlights important dates for test prep and registration. It's exactly what I needed. I can move forward more informed and confident that when the time comes, my sons will be ready to apply to the colleges of their choice… I praise God for having provided me with the guidance and support I need to homeschool high school with confidence and direction, and not with panic and fear."
~Virginia, California

"I am SO thankful to Aiming Higher for the invaluable help given to us in putting together our son's college documents! Jeannette helped me tailor his documents so that colleges would see who my son really is, and helped me to focus on what would help reach HIS goals. Her practical advice and experience helped us avoid a lot of unnecessary energy, time, and money. She explained the documents I needed and how to construct them, and then checked all of them over before they were submitted. This gave my son and me so much confidence in the process and I'm positive it was instrumental in securing for him a wonderful scholarship at a school we had only dreamed he might attend (Boston University)."
~Terri, Colorado

"I cannot imagine what school I would now be waiting to attend were it not for Aiming Higher's aid. Sending in quality paperwork and essays proves that homeschoolers can indeed accomplish! I applied to eight post-secondary schools, most of them in the upper echelon of music and academics, and each required a different sort of application and supplements.

Attending my dream university AND a prestigious conservatory simultaneously through a five-year dual degree program has greatly heightened my excitement for the coming years! Johns Hopkins is a renowned research school, one that fulfills my passion for exploring the unknown. Peabody Conservatory stands as the oldest music conservatory in America and as one of the world's finest. Together, they will provide the learning opportunity of a lifetime.

I take off my hat to Mrs. Webb and her associates. They are highly trained, definitely experienced, and unceasingly helpful. I would recommend Aiming Higher Consultants to anyone seriously considering post-secondary education."
~Michael, California

called to influence

A New Approach to Life, Education and College Admissions

by Jeannette Webb & Austin Webb

PRAIRIE SONG
PUBLISHING

Called to Influence: A New Approach to Life, Education and College Admissions

Copyright © 2010 by Jeannette Webb and Austin Webb (book design and formatting). Articles written by Jeannette Webb and Austin Webb and copyright © 2005-2010 Home Life, Inc. Used by permission.

All rights reserved. No part of this book may be used or reproduced or transmitted in any form or by any means, electronic or mechanical, including photocopying and recording, or by any information storage and retrieval system, without permission in writing from the publisher except in the case of brief quotations embodied in critical articles or reviews.

Designed and Published in the United States of America by:
Prairie Song Publishing
9437 N. 2340 Road
Custer City, Oklahoma 73639

Cover design and layout by Melanie Webb, www.modostrategy.com

Library of Congress Control Number: 2010924607
ISBN 978-0-9844623-0-8

FIRST EDITION

acknowledgments

We wish to thank . . .

. . . . all the families who have followed our writing and who have given us the pleasure of walking alongside them in their journey through high school planning and college applications. It has been a privilege.

. . . . Mary Pride, for seeing potential in a high school senior's storytelling ability and giving him a voice in *Practical Homeschooling* magazine.

. . . Rick Webb, our husband and father who often worked two or three jobs at a time so we could have the freedom to live the grand experiment called Home Education. We love you!

Jeannette and Austin Webb
Custer City, Oklahoma
April 2010

contents

1 Setting Your Sights High 01
Austin: Getting into a Top College 01

2 Laying the Groundwork 05
Jeannette: SAT Prep for First Grade? 05

Jeannette: How I Trained my Children to Be Leaders 08

Jeannette & Austin: The Gift of a Mentor 12

Jeannette: Parents as Mentors 16

Jeannette: Raising Gifted Children Right 21

Austin: Regaining Our Pioneer Spirit: Staying Home and Standing Out 29

3 Navigating High School 33
Jeannette: The Freshman Year of High School: Keep it Real 33

Jeannette: The Sophomore Year of High School: Emerging Butterflies 38

Jeannette: The Critical Junior Year 43

Jeannette: Senior Year: The Final Lap 46

4 Building an Academic Profile 51
Austin: Turbo-charge Your High School Academics 51

Jeannette & Natalie: PSAT/SAT/ACT and National Merit 55

Austin: Test Savvy 60

5 Building an Extracurricular Profile 65

Austin: Choosing the Best High School Activities 65

Jeannette: Building a College Résumé 69

6 Applying to College 73

Jeannette: How to Pick a College 73

Austin: Selling Colleges on You 78

Jeannette: The College Application 82

Austin: Your College Admissions Essay 87

Jeannette: Essays the Bring Home the Bacon 91

Jeannette: The Counselor Letter 94

Austin: Getting Great College Recommendations 98

Austin: College Interviews 102

7 Once You Get There 107

Austin: How Dangerous is College? 107

About the Authors 114
Resources 117

introduction

The articles in this book represent a four-year period in our lives, one filled with absolute awe at what God had done. He opened doors we never thought possible and made a way for us to go through them. You see, when we made the decision years ago to live off the grid, to home educate, to say "no" to tons of résumé builders, to live a family-focused life, to ignore what everyone else said we needed to be doing, we weren't even sure our children could get into college or whether we could pay for it if they did.

Our goal was to raise children who would influence others, not be influenced by the culture. It is a joy to see them now functioning as strong beacon lights in the cultural epicenters that are America's top colleges.

Our work through Aiming Higher Consultants has allowed us to meet some of the most outstanding Christian young people in America today. It has been delightful to assist these students that God has "Called to Influence."

We hope this book gives you the courage to break the rules and live the unique life that God has called your family to live. Blessings!

setting your sights high

Getting Into a Top College

Austin: I'm still surprised by all that transpired in my senior year of high school. For a long time my family wasn't sure if we could pay for college or even if a serious college would admit me. Having grown up homeschooled on an isolated farm in western Oklahoma, I took only one formal class and didn't lay eyes on a standardized test until the age of 17. Needless to say, I was somewhat surprised when Harvard, MIT, and other schools started shelling out money in airfares to recruitment events and offering huge financial aid packages trying to recruit me.

You've probably heard of the Ivies (Harvard, Yale, Princeton, etc.), the Institutes of Technology (MIT, Caltech), and private universities such as Rice, Duke, and Stanford. They are sometimes referred to collectively as the "top colleges." Most people are frightened off by rumors of impossible admissions standards or high cost. I certainly was intimidated initially, but a series of events changed my perspective. I would like to share what I learned and show you how a top college just might be in your future.

Boxes to be Checked
The first step in the process is to figure out what you want by comparing your goals with what specific colleges offer. There are any number of characteristics you might consider for a given college, but we will discuss only quality of education, atmosphere, affordability, and post-college employability.

Grey Matters
All degrees are not created equal, either in terms of academics or real world experience. Many factors affect the quality of education at a particular institution. Some are purely academic, such as class size, quality of teaching, interaction with students and professors, and the availability of academic resources (libraries, labs, etc.). Other aspects are more practical, such as opportunities for research, internships, and networking. On both counts, the top colleges generally excel due to

their huge endowments and strong networks of global relationships. I chose to attend my particular college not only for the academics but also the fact that it will provide me the chance to learn from and work with some of the greatest scientists alive. If you are willing to work hard and keep your eyes open, similar opportunities may be presented to you.

The Proper Care and Feeding of Social Animals

Even with engrossing academics, four years is still a long time. Be sure to spend it with students you like in an atmosphere that you enjoy. One of the best ways to understand the environment at a particular college (short of visiting it) is to read a current copy of the ISI Guide, *Choosing the Right College: The Whole Truth About America's Top Schools*. This guide profiles America's top schools, examining academic, social, and political life from a conservative vantage point. I found it to be extremely helpful in getting a feel for each institution. Given that homeschoolers tend to be more mature, disciplined, and intellectually serious than average, they will probably fit in much better with their peers at a top college than in most other institutions. Through college programs, I've made many friends who are bound for top colleges. Having spent most of my life as a social/academic misfit, it was a great joy to find students who shared my passion for knowledge and my sense of fun. They have greatly broadened both my social and intellectual horizons and will continue to do so through my college years.

> "Many families at the lower end of the middle class will find that a top college is their cheapest option."

Don't misunderstand, the atmosphere at most institutions (including most Christian universities) has the potential to poison a student's faith. Attending a top college is NOT for the intellectually lazy or the spiritually immature. The academics will push you to your limits. Your peers and professors will test your spiritual grounding. While it is a sobering prospect, I'm not worried because I have already been through boot camp. I am not going to college to be influenced, but to influence. That's why I've spent all these years homeschooling.

Piggy Bank Protection

One myth about attending a top college is that it is prohibitively expensive. While I can't speak for all cases, this is not a rule. In fact, many families at the lower end of the middle class will find that a top college is their cheapest option. The "sticker price" of a top college is high, but because of large endowments, colleges are often willing to shell out significant financial aid to desirable students. The top colleges to which I was admitted paid for virtually everything except my books and some personal expenses. It's nice to know I won't have to live on oatmeal and squirrels from the park for the next four years.

The Rat Race

The ultimate purpose of higher education (for most of us) is to get a job. I plan on getting married, having children, and homeschooling (in that order) one of these days, so remunerative employment is rather important. One question you need to ask yourself concerning higher education and its role in your future is "how many degrees do I need to get the job I want?" For fields such as engineering, information technology, and some areas of corporate business and finance, a bachelor's degree will suffice, though postgraduate degrees are becoming more common. For those with only undergraduate degrees, the alma mater's reputation can have a substantial effect on starting salary. For law, medicine, science, senior corporate positions, and virtually any career in academia, postgraduate degrees are required and the quality of undergraduate education can help with placement into a prestigious graduate or professional schools. Further, a top college can provide undergraduate research and internship experience that can give you an important edge during and after postgraduate study. It's good to get experience early, because if you aren't prepared you won't be able to take advantage of opportunities that present themselves.

Planning and Other Necessary Evils

Future columns will give a detailed outline of the application process, including taking tests, planning high school academics and extracurriculars, writing effective essays, and interviewing successfully. I can't stress enough that the process takes a great deal of effort and is very time consuming. If anything I have said has resonated with you and if you think a top college might be of interest, I encourage you to start early. Even if your child isn't yet in high school, it is important to understand college admissions so you can make informed decisions and start planning. If you are a parent you will find that the admissions game is much different today than it was when you were applying to college. The best way to start is by reading *How To Get Into The Top Colleges* by Richard Montauk and Krista Klein. This book is clear, extremely thorough, and offers great insight into the admissions process. It will help you to make the most of high school and to avoid getting blindsided.

"Admission to a world-class university brightened this farm boy's future and it could do the same for you."

A Final Word(s)

I hope this column has encouraged you to consider some new options. I did, and it has opened up possibilities beyond my wildest dreams. The road there isn't easy, but the rewards at the end are great. As a homeschooling student or parent, you've invested a lot in education. Don't let that go by the wayside when homeschooling ends. Take the time to consider all your options and pick the best one. Admission to a world-class university brightened this farm boy's future and it could do the same for you.

Notes:

laying the groundwork

SAT Prep for First Grade?

Jeannette: I was deeply saddened when I read the September 11, 2006 issue of MSNBC.com, in which an article entitled "The New First Grade: Too Much Too Soon?" detailed the pressures facing today's youngest students - incredible expectations, high-stakes testing, after-school tutoring, and on and on ... for five-year-olds!

It's been a long time since my children were five. My hair is graying and my first homeschool experiment now stands 6'2" and towers over me. He achieved everything that the yuppie parents in the MSNBC article want for their children – a perfect SAT score, the outstanding National Merit Scholar in the U.S. in science and math, award-winning high school science research, even a trip to the White House to be recognized by President Bush. He is now studying math and physics at one of the most prestigious universities in the world. And yet, as my mind flits back over the years, his five-year-old life looked very different than today's high-pressure childhood.

> "We do begin preparation for the SAT in first grade, but in a way that would confound those wise in the world."

Childhood Preparation
When my son was five we baked lots of cookies together, learning to measure and count. He snuggled in my lap often through the day while we read stories aloud. We chased fireflies in the pasture, explored the canyons behind our house, splashed in the stream, and stretched out on

the trampoline as we watched the stars at night. We listened to classical music as we cleaned the house together and told stories as we weeded the garden. We talked. A lot.

The elementary years were filled with home-based activities to help the children develop communication skills (both written and verbal), to instill discipline by playing a musical instrument, to expand their knowledge of the world around them by reading widely and taking appropriate field trips. As we grew into the junior high years we added leadership training to the mix of academics, discussions of current events, and volunteering.

Tough Love

We did pursue excellence throughout the years, but it was an excellence where love set the curve. Love knew when to push and when to cancel school for the day. Love knew when it needed to be perfect and when it was good enough. Love made each day a delight to explore and kept the excitement of learning alive. But love was also tough when it needed to be. Austin has shared in earlier articles that we worked hard to confront each child's weaknesses. In high school, we routinely pushed beyond academic and personal comfort zones. However, I was always attuned to each child's stress level and intervened before they reached the threshold. I would send them outside to jog a few miles or to the lawn chair with a good book to allow them time to regroup. Sometimes I had to eliminate wonderful activities or say no to great opportunities.

Perhaps here is the difference. I'm sure the driven parents mentioned in the article love their children. They want what is best for them. But I have a hunch that when we are separated from our children for hours a day that somehow we lose touch with the essence of each individual child. When we get out of the habit of practicing our parenting (by turning it over to paid professionals) we slowly lose confidence in our ability to make these critical judgment calls. Gradually we become estranged from our maturing children and eventually consider it to be a normal state of affairs when we can no longer connect with their souls. We are fearful of taking a tough stance, of making a countercultural decision that will be unpopular with this alien in our midst.

> "It is so very simple and yet it will demand all we have to give."

Homeschool Caution

Before homeschooling parents begin to pat themselves on the back, you must know that this same rift happens easily within our realm as well. When we allow too much of our children's lives to be superintended by homeschool co-ops, coaches, tutors, extracurriculars . . .we can wake up one morning and realize the chasm has grown too wide. We no longer know when to push or when to apply grace. Be forewarned that we homeschool moms tend to err on the side of grace. We expect too little of our high school students or we get overwhelmed and very little school happens at all. Our children will suffer in adulthood if we set the bar too low.

The Answer is Yes

If your children have had a rich and stimulating elementary/junior high existence, they will have the mental and physical resources to ramp up quickly for the demands of high school. In truth, we do begin preparation for the SAT in first grade, but in a way that would confound those wise in the world. We prepare our children for so much more than the SAT by nurturing curiosity, giving them time to think, reading, talking, building relationships, developing discipline, teaching them to work, modeling how to learn, speaking vision into their lives, and, most importantly, expecting the best that each child has to offer. It is so very simple and yet it will demand all we have to give.

> **Austin:** After living for several years in a community of the world's most brilliant minds, I have come to the conclusion that you can't produce a functional, successful person by parental pressure or attempts to artificially accelerate education. The most academically successful people I know who are actually able to function outside of home are the products of supportive families that provided intellectual resources without undue amounts of pressure to succeed. Whether you start college at 8 or at 20 (I have known profoundly brilliant people in both categories), the important thing is that the drive comes primarily from the student and that the family provides support. Piling on tests and "enrichment activities" can stamp out creativity and work against the acquisition of real knowledge and competence.

Notes:

How I Trained My Children to Be Leaders

Jeannette: Top colleges are looking for leaders who can take full advantage of the opportunities a good college will give them. Of course, they don't fill their whole class with leaders (they are also looking for humanitarians, go-getters, and entrepreneurs) but if you look carefully at the list, leadership qualities really function in all the categories - drive, desire to fix problems, motivation, the ability to think outside the box, and the gift of understanding and managing people.

Early Training

One of my students was a born leader and I just had to refine her plans. My other student was a reluctant leader who had to be coached in baby steps for years. We began by accepting leadership responsibilities as a family and each child would have their own tiny roles. We practiced a lot. For example, when an important phone conversation was coming up, we talked about it ahead of time and then analyzed the conversation afterward to see how it could have been more effective. They helped me organize homeschool

> "I wanted to shake my children up and see what they were made of."

support group meetings and shadowed us at community meetings or events. To teach them public speaking and presentation skills, I started a communications club for our homeschool group, then volunteered my son to teach small merit badge lessons at Boy Scout meetings.

As they became more mature, I began to turn over increasing responsibility. When my kids hit a snag, I waited for them to figure out the problem first before I jumped in with solutions. An unexpected bonus is that when kids have helped organize events, they take into adulthood an appreciation for the work involved in any organization. They are grateful to others who expend time in their behalf.

It is important to understand that volunteering is not leadership, but it does help children see what leadership entails so that it is a natural progression as they work their way up the ladder.

Grownup Leadership

In our school, it was required that each student tackle a huge leadership project before they graduated. Leadership training was just as important (but not more important) than Calculus. While it may sound harsh, I wanted to shake my children up and see what they were made of. Through the years I have learned that when kids have real responsibilities, when someone is depending on them, when someone might suffer if they don't do their job, the experience fundamentally changes them. I never set my children up to fail, but I made the bar high enough that failure was a possibility. It is risky, but I wanted to be there to catch them if they botched an activity. It would be devastating for that to occur in college when they are far from home.

Watching my children perform in leadership roles also gives me a chance to see if they maintain grace under pressure, if they remain loving when others are not loving to them. This is one of the few ways to really see if the years of character training actually worked. When they hit the wall, will they crumble and remain in a heap or will they get up and figure out how to work smarter next time? Did the experience damage their faith or strengthen it? These are important things to know before we send our kids into the war zone that is college.

Concert for Life
Let me give you an example of a leadership project that stretched my youngest student. When Natalie heard that our local Pregnancy Care Center ministry needed funds for an ultrasound machine, she came up with a plan to organize a benefit concert. She'd never seen it done before, but she was convinced that she could pull it off even though she was only 16. She requested a slot on the board meeting agenda and proceeded to stun board members with her unusual plan. She secured the largest church in town as the venue and contacted the music ministers of all area churches for performers from their congregations. She invited Christian music professors at the local college to participate as well. She asked each performer to be responsible for getting their church family to come. The final product was a wild mix of classical, instrumental, a capella, Christian contemporary, and praise music.

She convinced the local radio tycoon to give her free air time to run commercials that she wrote and produced, persuaded all the local printing companies to donate materials for the ad campaign she designed, and promoted the concert to local media (appearing live on radio programs and interviewing with newspaper reporters). She designed the short program that played before the concert telling about the Center's work and facts about the baby growing in the womb. She organized and performed in a piano trio with two university professors, worked with the sound technician and set-up crew, and emceed the concert. Natalie galvanized the community and the night of the concert there was a great turnout. The funds helped finance new equipment for the center, provided training for staff and board members, and helped stabilize the budget.

Basically, this young girl received great training in advertising, sales, and management. She learned important lessons about herself and her ability to deal with the organizational issues that such a huge project presented. Most adults would never attempt a leadership feat like this one; however, for my 16-year-old daughter, it was just another stretching experience. She was ready for the challenge because I started giving her important work to do as a toddler. Therefore, she came to the job with 14 years of experience under her belt.

Choices, choices . . . .
It seems that homeschoolers operate at opposite ends of the continuum regarding leadership. Either they overcompensate with leadership/extracurricular activities hoping admissions officers will ignore subpar academics and test scores or they forget the leadership component altogether and function only in the academic realm, hoping admissions officers will overlook the fact that their lives are one-dimensional. Either choice is a dangerous one, not only for college admissions, but for holistic development.

> "We need to look past all the *good* activities and select only the fraction that are truly excellent —those that will stretch our children and make a difference in our world."

I need to be upfront here and share with you that we NEVER EVER did any cocurricular, extracurricular, or leadership project so it would look good on a résumé or college application. I think Solomon would call that striving after the wind. This kind of foolishness teaches our students the wrong priorities and will eventually erode family cohesiveness. When all the individuals in a family are each chasing after multitudes of impressive activities, we are no longer operating as a family unit moving toward our particular goals. We lose touch with each other in the chaos of every day.

To avoid this, the activities and leadership ventures of our family were chosen to broaden existing gifts or strengthen a weakness that would hamper our children in the pursuit of their dreams. It was also important that our choices benefited the community in a real way.

We rarely did more than 2 or 3 things in a given year, often doing most of the work for a leadership project in the summer. The few activities we chose were pursued at a high level. After that goal was achieved, we usually moved on to another challenge. It is important that we not allow our students to get stuck in an activity rut. Once a student has mastered something and made a contribution, there is no reason to continue repeating the same lessons year after year.

Things to Remember

As parents, we need to use discretion when choosing how our children will invest their time. We need to look past all the good activities and select only the fraction that are truly excellent - those that will stretch our children and make a difference in our world. We only have a few years to guide this young life that has been entrusted to us. While it takes foresight and much effort on the parent's part, raising leaders for the kingdom is worth our sacrifice.

Notes:

The Gift of a Mentor

Jeannette: I'm convinced that God has a sense of humor. To prove it, he gave me, a mathematical midget, two children with quantitative minds that delight in math/science/engineering. I would be lying if I told you I accepted it calmly. Late at night I cried, I whined, I begged God to let me off the hook for educating these kids through high school. To make a long story short, He didn't give me a reprieve, but He did give a peace and He opened my eyes to possibilities that had been right in front of me all along.

Finding Help
When my 10-year-old son's knowledge of chemistry and resulting questions passed my own, in desperation I went to one of the elders in our church who just happened to be the head of the chemistry and physics department at our local university. I begged him for a book that I could read to get myself up to speed. Being both wise and kind, he suggested I drop Austin off at his office one day a week. He had some free time and was willing to answer his questions. It was the start of a mentoring friendship that would last for years and is, in fact, still going.

Austin: *A Tribute* (printed in the program for Austin's high school graduation, 2004)
It was a clear, fall day. The large windows in the college lab admitted streams of powerful, undiluted light. It seemed to make the test tubes and beakers in front of me glow. I was about ten at the time, perched high atop a lab stool and focused on a chemical experiment. My mentor stood nearby, keeping an eye on the procedure and patiently answering my effervescent stream of questions. In a burst of enthusiasm, I asked, "Do you think I could be a chemical engineer?" "Yes," he replied, "but you could also be a physicist." That thought was locked away in my memory, to be retrieved and pondered. Eventually, it became a dream.

I came to Dr. Sonobe as a young boy, bursting with questions. Most people didn't know what to do with me. Dr. Sonobe, however, took my ramblings as a matter of course. Though most chairs of university physics and chemistry departments wouldn't have deigned to put up with an erratic 10-year-old, he patiently explained concepts, helped me with numerous experiments, and answered the multitudes of questions I came up with, no matter what the topic, no matter how far off topic. Whatever I was interested in, he had time to discuss.

I grew older and my aspirations started to solidify. I delved deeper into the sciences and he gave suggestions for my course of study. As my interests expanded, he helped me with other endeavors. When I pursued high school and college studies, Dr. Sonobe was ready to help. Once, when living out of state, I lacked access to equipment and materials I needed to complete some labs. Dr. Sonobe offered to help and made the time consuming arrangements. I spent a solid week of 8-9 hour days in his lab, much of that time with his assistance and guidance. He invited me to stay with his family and in the evenings we discussed the day's experiments and their implications, current research topics in science, and local news. Years ago, he had opened my eyes to what I could become. Now he was assisting me in a very practical way to prepare for that endeavor.

Dr. Sonobe has been my teacher, mentor, and friend for almost a decade now. From the time when I needed a stool to reach the lab bench, to now, at my current height of 6'2", from my youthful scientific ramblings to my present focused work towards a scientific career, he has been there, helping and affirming.

There is certainly the temptation to be proud of where I am, to say "look what I did" or think of myself as somehow a self-made man, but it wouldn't be true. Probably no one who ever lived can say that they achieved purely by virtue of their own faculties and volition. If the truth be known, we are all much indebted to fellow human beings who offered a helping hand even though no obligation compelled them. I owe much to many, but few more than Dr. Sonobe who taught me by example to look beyond present circumstances and see what might be. Many years ago he pointed out distant possibilities on the horizon and has walked beside me on the journey ever since. •

Musical Mentors

My daughter's relationship with her mentors was much shorter lived. We relocated for one year to Colorado where she met a musician couple who took her to their hearts. He was her violin teacher and orchestra conductor. She taught Natalie violin pedagogy to enable her to teach her own students. We spent a great deal of time in their company. This showed my daughter how hard musicians work to survive - studios of 30 or more children who need weekly lessons, professional duties as members of an orchestra, and random gigs (playing at weddings or events) for extra money. After one particularly long weekend, the wife collapsed in a chair and said, "Don't do what I've done! I play with men and women in our professional orchestra that are business people by day and make music at night. You have the ability to do that." Later he made a revealing statement when Natalie was performing a "for fun" piece at lesson, "How I miss getting to play for enjoyment. After teaching all day and working on music for the next performance, I don't have time to play music for pleasure anymore." Their transparency during that year was enlightening for my daughter. She began to consider relegating her music to a delightful avocation rather than her academic focus.

> "My son's relationship with his mentor propelled him forward to attain higher goals than we ever thought possible. My daughter's association with her mentors caused her to re-evaluate the direction of her life and choose a different path."

A Mentor's Gift

My son's relationship with his mentor propelled him forward to attain higher goals than we ever thought possible. My daughter's association with her mentors caused her to re-evaluate the direction of her life and choose a different path. These adults cared deeply about my children and gave advice that was pivotal to who they became.

A true mentor is a gift from God and we will be fortunate if we have two or three in a lifetime. As a parent, I cannot orchestrate this relationship as there has to be a spontaneous chemistry. However, I can look around me with new eyes at extended family, church family, and associates to see if there is someone possessing the skills I lack and/or who might take a special interest in my child. I have found that adults are usually eager to help a child with whom they share an interest. Some of these contacts will only result a meeting or two and will never develop into a mentoring relationship, but have, nonetheless, enriched the life of our student. You just never know what might be the beginning of a lifelong friendship.

Notes:

Parents as Mentors

Jeannette: Many parents are comfortable seeking outside mentors. It's tough, but most of us can humble ourselves enough to ask for help. However, when I suggest that we, as parents, should be the child's primary mentors, eyes start bugging and hands begin to shake. "But I'm not an expert! But I'm the mother of a teenage son! But, but…" These excuses are routine, but in light of scripture, pretty weak. After all, in Deuteronomy 6, the command is startlingly comprehensive. We are to teach when we sit in the house, when we walk by the way, when we lie down, and when we rise up. This commandment is given to me, the parent, with my weakness, my inabilities, my failures, my lack of confidence, my fatigue.

Parents as Mentors

I spent several years stumbling around in the dark before I came to the understanding that God gave my children to me for a reason. I had argued with Him for several years about the students he had given me - surely He was mistaken and they should have been born into a family that could further develop their innate talents. However, He made it clear to me that my skills were exactly what they needed. He promised to take care of the math and science (my weaknesses), but it was in my court to deal with both subject matter in which I had a specialty as well as gifts I possessed and skills I had developed (my strengths).

> "Most families today lead divergent lives - sleeping in the same house at night, but going alone in different cars to different activities by day. Their lives never really intersect."

A Parent's Tool Chest

When I stopped long enough to take an inventory of my abilities, I unearthed things that I thought belonged in my past, but God clearly thought I needed to be teaching today. Leadership and organization have always been a part of my life and with that came skills in public speaking, writing, interviewing, journalism, copy writing for radio, and political campaign strategizing. This may not sound like a big deal, but my oldest was an extreme introvert who really did not like people and who stuttered horribly in front of a crowd. We are talking a seemingly impossible mission here. Yet, fourteen years later, nobody would guess his secret. My son is an easy-going young man with a gentle leadership style. He has many friends, knows how to navigate social networks and speaks easily in front of groups. But how do you get there?

Parallel Lives

Most families today lead divergent lives - sleeping in the same house at night, but going alone in different cars to different activities by day. Their lives never really intersect. Sadly, this is true of many homeschooling families. To truly mentor our teens, we need parallel lives - working alongside each other accomplishing what needs to happen for the good of the family. When my children were little it meant weeding the garden or cleaning the house together, each having a different job but in close proximity so we could talk (and I could oversee). In the teen years it takes a different form. My daughter does schoolwork on the kitchen table as I work in the kitchen or at the nearby computer. I am there to answer questions (not usually school related). When Natalie is working at the computer on a project, I am nearby to proof emails, give advice, help her understand the dynamics of whatever group she's dealing with. We get in our exercise and a lot of discussion during our daily walk. When I'm organizing an activity, she is practicing her violin within hearing distance so I can call her in to proof my work or to get her input on my latest idea. Because we live in such an isolated location, all extracurricular activities are 2 hours away (too far for a young driver) so we also spend time in the car together and constantly discuss.

> "Instead of devoting themselves to contrived classroom simulations, they are operating in the real world. It just doesn't get any better than that!"

Choosing Real Life

Because my children have always shadowed me as I engage in life, by late junior high they are ready for the real thing. We work as a family to create or improve organizations and influence our community. I start handing over increasing responsibilities as their development allows. I teach them to network, to navigate political structures, to deal with the media. I routinely lead them outside their comfort zone. They are educated in organizational management and community involvement and are expected to be servant leaders.

As teens, they have the maturity to learn quickly and be entrusted with much. Working in parallel transfers easily to the public square. In the Capitol, we divide and conquer, cell phones handy. On political campaigns, I'm driving the van as they jump out the side doors to distribute campaign literature. In board meetings, I'm at the back of the room ready to help if they get in over their heads while making a presentation. Instead of devoting themselves to contrived classroom simulations, they are operating in the real world. It just doesn't get any better than that!

Have Courage

The hard part is that when I commit to really walk the road alongside my young disciples, my life becomes uncomfortably transparent. As I look at my children and see something unacceptable, it is often a reflection of my own weakness and something I have to correct in myself before I can expect better behavior of them. It is a humbling experience when the Lord uses my offspring to bring a character flaw to my attention, but I'm a better woman today for having chosen the homeschool road.

The Rewards

I have learned recently that the secretaries of many American physicists receive hardship pay because their bosses are so arrogant and horrible to deal with. I look up at my caring and compassionate son and have to laugh at the grand design God had for our family. So that was why Austin was given to me instead of to a scientific parent! He knew all along it would take my strong personality and every skill at my disposal to keep him humble and lead him beyond the very limiting confines of his geek comfort zone.

> "My job as a parent is not to replicate myself, but to teach my children everything I know and find other mentors or instructors to teach them the things I don't. It is to look at my children with honest eyes and choose daily to correct weaknesses that will impede them in the real world."

Each Family Unique

The life of your family will look totally different from mine. Each family is uniquely gifted to carry out their particular mission on this earth. Each member is designed to complement and strengthen the others. Trust me, you have gifts and skills that are exactly what your children will need to truly flourish.

My job as a parent is not to replicate myself, but to teach my children everything I know and find other mentors or instructors to teach them the things I don't. It is to look at my children with honest eyes and choose daily to correct weaknesses that will impede them in the real world. Trained in this way, they can then stand on my shoulders as they begin their adult life and go farther than I ever dreamed of going in mine.

Are you ready for the challenge of partnering with God to help your children be the best they can be? It's a wild ride, but the most exciting one you'll ever take.

Austin: From time to time I hear people advocating a hands-off parenting style. This school of thought (if it's coherent enough to be called that) dictates parental non-judgementalism with the justification that "kids need to make and learn from their own mistakes." While the last statement is to some extent true, it is unwise to take this as an excuse to avoid passing on knowledge that could induce the desired learning without the need to suffer from an unnecessary mistake. Being human, we're going to make errors anyway. It makes sense to at least be original about it and not repeat what's already been done.

A parent who is an effective mentor can give their children the benefit of wisdom and experience beyond what their short years would normally permit. My parents' willingness to add their strengths to my own (without trying to change who I was) allowed me to assume adult responsibilities at a young age and enter college vastly better adjusted than I would have otherwise. It was one of the greatest gifts anyone has ever given me.

Notes:

Raising Gifted Children Right

Jeannette: Every so often a child comes along that captures the imagination of those outside his or her immediate family. Whether a gifted athlete or an academic genius, this child is recognized as something special and people begin to talk. However, too often giftedness is not handled well and instead of being an asset to propel our child toward great things, it becomes a millstone that threatens to drown their very soul.

Scary Examples
Examples abound: the math prodigy who started studying differential equations at age 10 and then flunks out of his dream college in his late teens because he's too busy playing video games; the daughter of a professor (who ironically taught college classes on giftedness) with an off-the-charts IQ that wasted her young adulthood meditating in Tibet in a vain attempt to find the meaning of life; the all-star athlete who had it all and lost it to drugs and immorality; the inspired actor who gets disoriented in the shallowness of the Hollywood scene. So much promise. Such a huge waste.

Parenting in the Twilight Zone
Parenting a gifted child will require everything we have to give and sometimes even more. It will necessitate a dependence on our heavenly Father for guidance when the way is no longer clear. While our child's gift will probably surpass our ability in one particular area, we have the advantage of life experience and wisdom that they do not possess. Never forget that. As homeschoolers, we have a unique 24/7 opportunity to mentor gifted children so they do not stumble in the limelight. It's not easy, but here are some foundations upon which to build.

Keep Your Mouth Shut
Don't ever talk about your child's gifts/IQ in their presence. EVER! I am amazed at the parents who ramble on and on about their child's exceptional gifts in front of them. I get an earful of how brilliant, how wonderful, how talented… while the tiny child is there absorbing the fact that their parents idolize them. At an early age, we are on dangerous ground already. Take a minute to re-read Exodus 20. We must own that idolatry is sin.

It is an easy trap to fall into. (After all, it proves that our homeschooling is successful. Right? Perhaps they are gifted because we homeschool?) We are so enraptured that we have special kids that we bore others and endanger our child.

When they are old enough to figure out for themselves that they are special, they are old enough to understand the responsibilities involved. My son was fifteen when a friend spoke aloud for the first time of his giftedness and took him by surprise. When he approached me for validation, we had a wonderful discussion about the fact that much would be expected of him because God had entrusted him with much. It was a humbling experience rather than a detrimental inflation of his ego.

For this reason, I am very hesitant about the proliferation of talent searches and gifted ID programs. Basically many of these things are money-makers and I'm not convinced it is helpful to have the information (or the label) they provide. I have found that labels are seldom beneficial whether they tell us that a child is gifted, normal, ADD, or learning disabled. While this knowledge should be useful to help us deal with reality and correct problems, parents seldom handle this information well and tend to brandish the label as a trophy or as an excuse.

> "It doesn't take long at all for them to develop the attitude that life owes them entertainment and Starbucks coffee."

Neither should we talk about our own inabilities in front of our children. During one difficult season, I was feeling totally inadequate with this homeschool thing. I made a comment to my father (in front of my young children) that I was not smart enough to do this. Normally slow to share his opinions, my father promptly took me to another room and gave me a "talking to" that I have never forgotten. Basically he told me that my children would not submit to my teaching or my leadership if I caused them to lose confidence in me. I was the adult and I needed to start acting like one. Ouch!

There does come a time when our teens have the maturity that allows us to share more openly about our struggles, but that comes much later.

Seek Service
Service is a fundamental part of the Christian lifestyle. Further, I suggest that it is absolutely essential for gifted children. They need to be routinely called outside themselves for the benefit of someone else. They need to figure out that life is about serving others, not about them. They need to serve their family daily. They should be expected to make personal sacrifices for the benefit of all.

I am not talking about service in the area of their giftedness. A musician does not benefit from performing at a charity event - that just provides a bigger audience to praise her. A socially inept computer whiz learns nothing from spending time alone programming the church computer. While it goes without saying that our children should use their talents to serve others, we must also include sacrificial service outside their natural gifting that costs them something and keeps them humble. They need tough responsibilities that rest on their shoulders such that if they fail, someone suffers.

It is vital that we pursue service opportunities as a family. We need to be involved with our kids. This is where the real learning takes place. If you are a member of a huge, feel good church where everything is provided for you (i.e. multitudes of youth pastors to cater to young teens' every whim), don't expect your kid to learn what it means to be a servant leader. This common scenario will teach them the opposite - that it's all about them. It doesn't take long at all for them to develop the attitude that life owes them entertainment and Starbucks coffee.

My son was blessed beyond measure in that he had the daily example of a father with a servant's heart. Pious lip service will only turn intelligent kids into cynics. They need to see the real thing, over and over, in the lives of people they love. Austin saw this in his father. He also saw it in his mentor, a brilliant chemist and elder at our church who rolls up his sleeves to work with the rest of us. Knowing that this highly successful man took his turn at church scrubbing toilets and vacuuming carpet gave my son a perspective on what it means to wash others' feet that nothing else could.

Find Something Difficult

Because most things are so effortless for the gifted child, they are often totally unprepared to deal with something difficult. They are not used to having to wrestle with a concept or sweat to learn proper procedures. We need to be diligent to place things in their path that they bump into. Things that hurt. Why? Gifted kids need to be humbled. They need to learn how to learn.

Good parents naturally make huge sacrifices to push the envelope of their child's giftedness. It is fun and rewarding to watch a special child develop. It is a pleasure to open doors and make sacrifices because others see and applaud our efforts. But too many parents stop there. We must also make the enormous sacrifice to help them develop in the areas that are weak. This will be infinitely harder. We will often encounter an intense struggle and our efforts may not be rewarded for many years.

Perhaps the athlete needs tough academics that will really whip him. Maybe our talented musician needs to be pounded with rigorous speech and debate. Some kids may need hard, sweaty physical labor that makes for aching muscles. Some kids need stretching leadership or a gut-wrenching volunteer responsibility. Perhaps our student is weak socially and covers for it with an intellectual arrogance. We found the answer for this in a hard, unforgiving peer group. Boy Scouts taught our son valuable life lessons that his homeschooled Christian friends were too nice to dish out. Team sports could have been another avenue.

We must understand that when a child (or adult) is allowed to live solely within the bubble of their strength, it is easy to become arrogant toward lesser mortals. They rule their tiny kingdom and become tyrants. If, however, we pop the bubble and require them to live in places outside their strengths, they quickly learn that others have talents they do not. They become more realistic, kinder. They learn how to appreciate the strengths of others and how to get along with the rest of the world. They develop skills that come hard, but make them whole.

> "We decided to help our children keep life in perspective by having them spend most of their time in the adult world."

Beware a Lopsided Development
Perhaps another way of looking at this is a concept called four-fold development. Explained in the old-fashioned little volume *I Dare You!* by William H. Danforth of Ralston Purina fame, this framework sought a balanced approach to life. Using Luke 2: 52 as a foundation "And Jesus increased in wisdom and stature, and in favor with God and man," Danforth concluded that we should strive to grow in all four areas. He labeled them mental, physical, religious, and social. Keeping a balance between them allows for healthy growth and development.

It is foolish for parents (and potentially devastating for our child) to rely on a one-dimensional development. I have too often heard an adult tell their student "We'll just count on a sports scholarship. We don't need to worry about your SAT scores." I expect this type of limited thinking in teens, but am appalled to find it in so many adults.

What happens when we allow a child to function in only one area? If our child receives his self-worth from being the smartest person around, who is he when he finds himself outpaced by those of greater abilities? If "athlete" is how our child defines himself, who is he when injury or illness permanently forces him to the sidelines?

Gifts are Fragile

We must understand that gifts are fragile things. A head injury, even a moderate one, can permanently hamstring mathematical ability. A finger injury can capsize a musician. A torn ACL can end an athletic career. As adults, we should have the maturity to see the big picture throughout a lifetime and help our students understand this concept. When our children learn to see things in this light, they become better stewards of their gift. They learn it must be handled with care and held loosely. They become grateful that God entrusted them with it and learn to use it wisely.

This is one more reason that we must help our children develop skills outside their area of strength. Not only are they better prepared for life, but they are also able to sidestep into something else should their gift and passion suddenly be taken from them.

> "I'm convinced that we lose so many Christian kids in college because we send them off with a weak, emotion-based, borrowed faith that has never been tested by fire. We have made life too comfortable and easy for them."

Function in the Adult World

Intellectually gifted children will totally outdistance other kids in their peer group. They know more than the others and have a quicker wit. They are often bored with the usual "teen" interests and this can lead to either underachievement or egotism.

We decided to help our children keep life in perspective by having them spend most of their time in the adult world. One example of this is their attendance in adult Sunday School. Instead of being in class with teen dramas, cliques, crushes, and self-centered prayer requests, they were with intelligent adults studying hard things. Their class of treasured older friends contains the brilliant university provost as well as a line-worker at the local factory. They gain from both perspectives.

Learning by example to truly search out Scripture during hardship has kept my kids grounded. My children are in constant fellowship with these adult friends. We have faced together job loss, death, cancer, Multiple Sclerosis, Huntington's Disease, agonizing months waiting for an organ transplant, and teenagers gone astray. Because they watched these adults daily living out their faith in a pain-filled world, friendship evangelism was an easy step in college. My children's faith is not based on emotion or dependent on hordes of friends backing them up during a planned "outreach" event. They are comfortable walking alone for Christ.

> "Christ *did life together* with this rag tag group of immature young men and then turned them loose to change the world."

I'm convinced that we lose so many Christian kids in college because we send them off with a weak, emotion-based, borrowed faith that has never been tested by fire. We have made life too comfortable and easy for them. They don't know how to wrestle with Scripture or with hard things. Worse yet, we often just expect a carbon copy of what we profess. We give them lists of rules. We do not tolerate a different opinion. Tough questions are viewed as rebellion. Only when they parrot back the right verbiage, do we consider our job well done. Be forewarned that this style of parenting will backfire. If your children do not own their faith, college will make short work of them.

The unnerving thing about parenting a gifted child is their ability to see past our pretense. If we would bring them outside themselves to help them lead a balanced, complete life, we must be willing to go first: to be uncomfortable, to fail, to recognize our own weakness, and have the courage to confront it.

More than anything else in the homeschool lifestyle, this issue of spiritual maturity requires first that we be mature as parents. We must live with a transparency that gives our children insight into how to overcome their own personal and spiritual struggles. They can't learn this from their youth pastor or their coach or their peers. It can only come as you journey along the Deuteronomy road together - when you sit, when you walk, when you lie down, when you rise up. We cannot talk at our kids (especially gifted kids). We must roll up our sleeves and do life together. There must be a constant dialog with them, a learning together, working together, suffering together, and crying together. If we offer them anything less, we deserve their cynicism.

This side-by-side lifestyle allows me to hold up my gifted child when he stumbles. But the miracle is that it also allows him to catch me when I falter and thus develop his own muscles. Rather than fostering contempt, it creates a deep respect and tenderness in my almost adult child. It gives him the courage to face hard things. After all, he has seen me do it time and time again.

Walking the Talk

God has entrusted us with much when he gave us a gifted child. The responsibility is incredible. Just think of the temporal and eternal implications of parenting an exceptional child well. This child could use their gifts to literally change the world - finding the cure for cancer, building an organization to relieve world poverty, or writing a concerto that touches our hearts.

They say children don't come with an instruction book, but I beg to disagree. It's all right there in the Gospels: how to teach, how to lead, how to parent. Jesus did not hand his disciples a papyrus scroll and expect them to learn by memorizing it. He did not send them to youth group meetings at the synagogue. He walked in front of them sometimes and beside them sometimes, constantly talking, teaching, saying…

See?
Watch me.
Do as I do.
Let me explain.
Here is the secret of what you do not understand.

And then, he washed their feet.

Christ *did life together* with this rag tag group of immature young men and then turned them loose to change the world.

So there you have it - a method so very simple and yet so uncomfortably radical. This paradox requires us to lose our lives in order that our children find Life. If we persist in our selfishness, we risk losing our gifted children altogether. Eventually, a character flaw will overwhelm their gift and the loss will ripple throughout eternity.

We are the adults. It's time to start acting like it.

Notes:

Regaining Our Pioneer Spirit: Staying Home and Standing Out

Austin: I'm a history buff like many other homeschoolers and I am particularly fascinated by the history of the homeschool movement. In my observation, what once made homeschoolers distinctive was a special ethos that could be called a pioneer mentality. Basically, it was a steadfast dedication to family, home education, individual initiative, the creation of opportunity, and to ignoring what the rest of the world thought we needed to be doing. It's what kept that first generation of homeschoolers going in spite of the fact that they could be arrested and jailed at any time, the complete absence of pre-packaged homeschool curricula, and the harsh reality that homeschoolers weren't allowed to compete in public school sports. This mind set built the modern homeschool movement and, I suspect, will be required to keep that movement viable. At least, it worked for my family.

A Family's Story
If such a thing as a pioneering spirit exists, it couldn't find a better home than the corner of rural Oklahoma where I grew up. Though it might have seemed a less than ideal situation as opportunities for low-income homeschool families were scarce, I wouldn't have had it any other way.

My family has always been very close. We don't lead separate lives. Whenever something needs to be done, we all pitch in until it is finished and insofar as is possible, we do activities as a family and keep outside commitments from encroaching on our time together. Whenever we need something, we create it. Over the years, my family has started (or helped start) a homeschool group, three speech and debate clubs, a Boy Scout Troop, and a state chapter of TeenPact Leadership School.

This was made possible because our homeschool relied almost completely on self-study and Socratic dialogue. I did have a mentor to whom I owe much, and I took one outside class over the internet which was very helpful. Other than that I learned from books (real books, no textbooks except for science/math) and informal conversations with my parents. As such, we weren't tied down by set schedules or deadlines and could drop whatever we were doing to take full advantage of any worthwhile opportunity that presented itself. When I worked with TeenPact, there were several months of every school year in which I gave up school entirely to fulfill my responsibilities. Similarly, if I was coming up on an important event, like my Eagle Project or a standardized test, I could shift classes for more preparation time. This was possible since we schooled year-round.

It would be nice to say that our philosophy included detailed plans for how everything would work and that we never doubted our choices; however, neither would be true. Things were often difficult and uncertain, but we hung on.

We kept building things and quietly honing skills. At 17, I applied for an extremely competitive summer research program (the Research Science Institute) at MIT. Against all odds, I made it in. After that came the scholarship and science competitions. I made it there, too. Then came the college applications. We'll just say that I'm attending my dream school this fall, essentially for free.

Standing Out

The successes I had weren't accidental or purely the result of ability. They were directly linked to the philosophy that had guided my family and me for all the years that came before. The lifestyle we led allowed me to sharpen valuable skills to an unusual degree and to prove that I had initiative, that I could overcome both external obstacles and my own weaknesses. These things were valuable for their own sake (which was why we did it that way in the first place), but they did not go unnoticed by colleges and scholarship programs. Tragically, though, it seems that just as my family realized how powerful this philosophy is, much of the homeschool community seems to be abandoning it.

A Heritage Lost

I think that one main reason many homeschoolers give up the historical homeschooling ethos is fear: fear of not doing it right, fear of messing the kids up, fear of high school calculus, etc. By letting these fears (which admittedly are natural enough) get the better of us, I'm afraid homeschoolers too often bail out and fall back to safe-seeming and conventional alternatives. In doing so, they throw away the independence, originality, and "apartness" that makes homeschooling special.

I'm no stranger to the fact that homeschooling can be a nerve-wracking experience. Are we doing the right thing? Will our kids be able to get into college? It's enough to make many parents farm the work out to co-ops, community colleges, public-school-at-home programs, youth groups, and tons of outside activities. Some even quit home education entirely and send their kids to a traditional high school. That might seem like the safe option, but is it?

Pioneering Proves Practical

Let's look at just one consideration: getting into college. The advantage of a more institutional approach to school and life is that, to a college, you look normal, like your peers. The disadvantage is that you look normal, like your peers. If you're applying to a top college, this is exactly the type of person that they reject.

But someone who has taken a risk, who has initiative and has done what others fear to do just might catch an admission officer's eye. In my experience, you don't need to take loads of college classes or be a part of every activity in the immediate universe. One friend of mine scored perfect fives on nearly thirty AP exams; another attended one of America's top prep schools. Still another completed most of a science degree at a local university before graduating high school. However, my homespun candidacy fared every bit as well as (and a few times, even better than) theirs when scrutinized by elite schools.

> "We are called to be a people 'set apart' for the Lord's service. Not to be uninvolved in the world around us, but to be special, to be a light that shines out through the crowd. This doesn't happen automatically, though. It means living intentionally. It means walking away from what feels safe. It means rolling up our sleeves and getting to work."

Now, I can't generalize my experience; everyone is different. However, staying independent and outside of the institutional box is a viable option if you're willing to take some risks and work hard.

The Big Picture

Every generation, including ours, sees the ascent of new threats to life and liberty. If our nation is to overcome the decay within and the enemies without, we will need strong, steadfast leaders. Many observers believe that the homeschooling movement may provide those leaders. However, that won't happen unless we stay tough and independent, unless we fight the temptation to go with the crowd and do what everyone else does. Don't assume that things will take care of themselves or that someone will hand opportunities to you. We have to take the initiative and create our own solutions.

We are called to be a people "set apart" for the Lord's service. Not to be uninvolved in the world around us, but to be special, to be a light that shines out through the crowd. This doesn't happen automatically, though. It means living intentionally. It means walking away from what feels safe. It means rolling up our sleeves and getting to work.

Notes:

navigating high school

The Freshman Year of High School: Keep it Real

Jeannette: Most of us waltz merrily along in the early years of homeschooling. Adulthood for our children seems so far away. Then, abruptly, sometime in the 8th grade year, we realize in a panic that high school starts NEXT YEAR!!!! I personally began waking up in a cold sweat. I bargained with God. Surely it was time now to put my eldest in "real" school?

Now that I am on the other side of the high school mountain, I am thankful we stayed the course. My children began high school with the immaturity of most freshmen, but over the course of four years became my adult friends, co-laborers, business partners, and advisors.

If you haven't already, this is the time to take stock of your lifestyle. More than anything else it is critical that you eliminate distractions from your child's life (and possibly from your own). Some distractions that keep our teens from "real" living are things like malling, recreational dating, spectator sports, etc. Add to that electronic time wasters like video games, television, Facebook, iPods, cell phones, and blogs. Even many homeschool teen groups or church youth groups encourage this distracted mindset that focuses on the trivial. These groups can also foster a deadly peer dependency. Our students begin to have the expectation that the world exists only to entertain them.

When people ask me what I did to help my children be successful, I have to be honest that it is not so much what we did, but what we didn't do. We walked away from the distractions to focus on what was real - real work, real academics, real service.

Real Work
Because of our financial situation, both of my children had to begin working outside the home at an early age (nine and eleven) to pay for their school books, classes, and personal activities like Boy Scouts, music lessons, instruments, etc. At the time, I was grieved that they had to work so hard, but in hindsight it was the best thing that could have happened. They learned early to efficiently

manage their time and they truly appreciate the privilege of getting to sit down and study. Perhaps most importantly, they did not have time to get caught up in frivolities like their friends did. Work experience taught them to take nothing for granted and gave them a solid sense of discipline.

It is very difficult for any child to be successful away from home unless they are able to control their use of time. I think work experience and the discipline of playing a musical instrument were crucial in forging this awareness for my students.

These lessons from the working world are best learned in middle school up through the freshman year. After that point, it is more important for college-bound students to focus on academics and test preparation during the school year and leave paid employment (away from home) for summer break.

Simple neighborhood tasks such as raking leaves or snow shoveling can be done at almost any age by children who are physically fit enough to do the work. For actual company-paid employment, however, state and federal labor regulations apply. Some laws prevent young children from working during public-school hours, even if they are working in the family business and are homeschooling. (Exception: a school "work study" program where the child learns skills and puts them to use, but receives no pay.) Other laws specify exactly what types of work preteens and young teens can do - it varies by age. Check out www.youthrules.dol.gov.

> "When people ask me what I did to help my children be successful, I have to be honest that it is not so much what we did, but what we didn't do."

Real Academics

As we move into the high school years, it is important for a parent to take the time to plan the remainder of the journey. Four years will go by in a heartbeat! Take time to read and research on the front end. Where might your child be headed? Is college in their future (and what type of college) or do you need to think about apprenticeships? Perhaps you need to think about including both. What career field do you think they might be headed toward? What are their strengths? What are their weaknesses? I always encourage parents to plan as though every child will go to college for the simple reason that many kids will change their minds toward the end of high school and suddenly want to pursue a degree. Even if they don't go on to college, they deserve an excellent and thorough high school education to prepare them for life and for educating their own children.

When facing the high school years, many parents who have been creative up to that point, suddenly grasp for things that seem safe, like homeschool co-ops or highly structured homeschool curriculum. What has been an innovative environment of learning suddenly becomes regimented and boring. In my observation, many homeschool co-ops produce a slacker mentality. Bright students will soon see through a dumbed down textbook or classroom busywork. They don't have to work hard, so they mentally drop out. This habit will be devastating in a competitive college environment. Unfortunately, these teen classes that we adults have created to help us feel more secure (and look more like the rest of the world) encourage a teen culture that entraps our young people into thinking they are less capable than they truly are. For a thought-provoking piece from one of the country's most respected educators on this subject, see *Practical Homeschooling* issue #37 interview with John Taylor Gatto.

> "Pursue real service in which your child impacts the community or another life."

When possible, my family chose to learn through real world experiences, not classes or textbooks. We covered high school history, government, language arts, and some science in a real way. My children wrote for publications, experienced government at the State Capitol, did science in a university research lab, learned history by taking field trips and reading living books, and honed communication skills by giving speeches to various groups. For upper level or AP science and math, textbooks are necessary, but because my kids loved to learn, the rigorous textbooks proved to be a fun challenge.

Many students need the freshman year to get caught up in math. If you think your student has the potential to apply to a top tier college or might want to take AP classes, they need to have completed Algebra II or geometry (depending on the order you take them) by the end of the ninth grade year. I also recommend tackling Biology this year (which means you need to be covering Earth Science or Physical Science in 8th grade). This gives you the freedom to advance quickly into tougher high school classes, AP courses, or college classes in the next few years. While there are some highly gifted students out there who are ready for AP and college classes at the freshman year, my two children were not.

Real Service

In my experience, most freshman are still a little rough around the edges. We were working hard at this age to overcome weaknesses and volunteering as a family in things that would help my children develop needed skills. I looked for stretching leadership opportunities, even though I knew my students would fail sometimes. This will be the most flexible year in high school, so try to concentrate as much leadership in this year as possible. For example, my son pushed hard and completed his Eagle Scout project by the end of his freshman year because he knew that it would become increasingly difficult to invest that much time at a later date.

If you are going to experiment with different kinds of activities to see where your student's strengths might be, this is the year for that. Unfortunately, many activities, contests, and clubs are fun, but pretty trivial. You can spend inordinate amounts of time on contrived situations that don't really teach your kid much academically, don't develop needed skills, don't benefit anyone else, and do disrupt your family life. Treat this kind of thing as a distraction and eliminate it. Pursue real service in which your child impacts the community or another life.

> "The choices we make now will determine whether those students enter the world as peer-dependent chameleons or as seasoned warriors."

After the freshman year, a college bound student won't have time to do a great deal of experimenting. It is a hard reality, but there are only so many hours in a day and to be successful, you will have to begin narrowing your focus.

The freshman year is an exciting beginning. I honestly believe that the high school years are the most important ones we will spend with our homeschool students. The choices we make now will determine whether those students enter the world as peer-dependent chameleons or as seasoned warriors. That is horribly blunt, but there is too much at stake to sugarcoat the truth.

Notes:

The Sophomore Year of High School: Emerging Butterflies

Jeannette: During my children's sophomore year in high school, I watched an interesting metamorphosis take place. Overnight it seemed, the chrysalis of childhood was shed and my young adults emerged. Light bulbs turned on. I believe the reason for this was that they bumped into rigorous upper level academics for the first time and the shake up forced them to mature. Now, you can choose to leave your children stuck in childhood (and lightweight academics is one way to do that), but the result is not pretty.

It's Time for AP Classes
For college-bound students, it is time to try an Advanced Placement class. This is a college level class taken in high school and followed by a 3-4 hour standardized test in May (offered at local schools). While not officially required, AP tests are becoming a standard expectation for admission to quality colleges.

My son knew he needed to take several AP classes in order to prove his abilities to a top college. After much research, (including several homeschool curriculums that claimed to be AP but on closer investigation proved inadequate), he decided to apply for a Biology class taught by Dr. Lauren Gross, Professor Emeritus of Johns Hopkins, taught through Pennsylvania Homeschoolers (www.pahomeschoolers.com/courses/). Dealing with an impeccably credentialed professor, a rigorous class load, and tons of practice essays prepared him to ace the AP test and to successfully compete for a slot at the prestigious Research Science Institute, where he worked in a neuroscience lab the summer after his junior year.

A word of caution is needed. There are many people cashing in on the online teaching market. Today there are all kinds of AP classes advertised, most of which look insufficient. Just because it is called AP does not mean it is equivalent to a college course or will prepare your student well.

Below are a few things to consider when evaluating the worth of an AP class.
- Check the instructor's qualifications in the field
- What is their research and teaching experience?
- How many years have they taught this particular class?
- How have their students performed on the AP exam in the past?
- Will they cover all topics on the exam? (check topics out on CollegeBoard.com)
- Will there be rigorous training in the essay portion of the test?

- Do they use the standard, rigorous texts in the field?
- How many hours are required for the class per week? A good AP class is generally worth the 10-20 hours weekly investment.
- Talk to former students about their experiences with the class

The CollegeBoard finally put its foot down regarding its "AP" trademark. Now, for a course to be called AP, the teacher must submit his credentials and syllabus to the CollegeBoard for approval. Don't call a class "AP" on your transcript unless it was sanctioned by the CollegeBoard and the student took the AP exam. Also, don't give your student an "A" on the transcript if they scored poorly on the AP exam. Admissions officers need to see that grades assigned by homeschool mothers can be trusted.

Instead of AP classes, some families will opt for dual credit at a local university. This can be a good option, but does tend to restrict your student's schedule more and there are the dangers of subjecting immature students to a college-age crowd. Further, the AP classes my students took far surpassed their options at our small local university.

"You can choose to leave your children stuck in childhood (and lightweight academics is one way to do that), but the result is not pretty."

SAT Subject Tests

Formerly known as SAT II tests, these one-hour tests assume a high school level mastery of the subject matter in math, science, English, languages, history, or social studies. Many colleges require at least 2 of these tests, some want as many as 6. These are offered 6 times a year at certified testing facilities, although the language tests with listening seem to be offered only in November. Check out CollegeBoard.com for more details than you probably want to know.

If you take an AP exam, take the SAT Subject test as well since it is so easy to dovetail your study time. For example, in May of their sophomore year, my children took the AP Biology exam and the SAT Subject test in Biology. I do recommend a test prep book and practice tests for each exam as they measure different things. My students try to take about 8 - 10 practice runs on any test they attempt because much of the secret to doing well is being familiar with the way questions are asked.

It is easiest to sit down at the first of the school year with a blank calendar and map out your study schedule and practice test runs. By getting into the habit of advance planning this year, your student will learn the discipline to schedule in the 6-7 tests they will have to take as juniors.

PSAT Practice
You are allowed to take the PSAT in October of your sophomore year as a test run. Your score will not be available to colleges, so it may be good practice for your students. However, my kids were not ready for this and I was unwilling to blow their confidence by attempting something prematurely. This is a judgment call for parents.

Catch up if Needed

"My husband and I saw this time in their lives as an investment that we were willing to fund. Never again will they have the time to study so diligently, to perfect musical abilities, to hone their skills that would grant them a place in the college of their dreams. However, had they been wasting time or making foolish choices, we would have immediately put them to work or upped the academic load."

If your student is behind academically, this is the year you must catch up if you want to be competitive in the college admission process. Many students are still behind in math or science and you must do whatever it takes to get finish the necessary classes. Some families hire tutors, allocate more time each day for critical subjects, or work through the summer to make it happen.

Especially in math, the student needs time for concepts to sink in before testing. In other words, don't finish up geometry the week before you take the PSAT. Ideally you should plan to finish all required math courses 6 months before taking any standardized tests like PSAT or SAT. You need to have time to play with concepts and be really comfortable with them. On the other hand, it is best to take science tests immediately following the class, as many of them require encyclopedic knowledge that tends to drain away with the passage of time. You need to finish 10th grade ready to take trig/pre-calculus and chemistry in the junior year.

Follow up Academic/Career Interests

If your student finds a new area of interest academically, pursue it. You just might find an unexpected career possibility or opportunities you never knew existed. My daughter loved the genetics portion of AP Biology and that summer asked a local professor to teach her the basics of molecular biology research. He was soon entrusting her with graduate level work.

Follow up Extracurricular Interests

Perhaps your student discovers a love of debate or public speaking. This is the age where those skills start to fall in place as well. These are real skills that will be useful as they navigate college and job interviews, give presentations, and engage in life. Just make sure you are pursing worthwhile activities and aren't dealing with distractions like we discussed in the last column.

Leadership Push

The sophomore year is the ideal time to develop a strong leadership record since the junior year is so hectic with college entrance tests. Both my children broke new leadership ground during this year. Austin built a statewide organization under the auspices of TeenPact Leadership School. With her best friend, Natalie created a nationwide debate network for isolated students. Single-handedly, she orchestrated a benefit concert to raise funds for a Pregnancy Care Center.

As in academics, we chose to let our children handle tough leadership projects as soon as they were developmentally ready. We were thrilled to watch them rise to the challenge and mature before our very eyes. As a bonus, they had built an incredible extracurricular record by the second year of high school.

What We Weren't Doing the 10th Grade Year

While most students this age are chomping at the bit to get their driver's license, both my students were so busy with academics, leadership, volunteering, and family life that they kept putting the driver's training on the back burner. While possibly not practical for some families, the choice to delay driving is worth your consideration. We all know the gruesome statistics of car accidents involving immature drivers, not to mention the fact that our insurance rates go out the roof for a newly licensed teen boy. I've seen tons of kids get caught in the distraction of working to pay for a car or gas and lose the most productive and precious years of their lives.

While you could say that continuing to chauffeur my children through high school was a burden, I found it to be a valuable time of connection with my academically busy kids. You have to take into account that we severely limit our outside activities and that most of what we do is done as a family anyway, so traveling together was a natural. We live in a very isolated area, so when we do something, it's normally a 2 - 4 hour drive. Those hours provided a welcome pause in our busy world. It gave us time to discuss and make heart connections.

During the high school years, many parents drop out of the picture. As a result, my children's friends leaned on me as a surrogate mom, knowing that I was always there in the background to help if needed. Because I was present and observing, I could see problems developing and nip them in the bud. I could give my children advice that was totally lacking in the lives of other teens (including homeschoolers). We became friends instead of adversaries.

This year (and the rest of high school) is not the time to let schoolwork suffer in order to work in a low wage job. While my children worked very hard when they were young, my husband and I saw this time in their lives as an investment that we were willing to fund. Never again will they have the time to study so diligently, to perfect musical abilities, to hone their skills that would grant them a place in the college of their dreams. However, had they been wasting time or making foolish choices, we would have immediately put them to work or upped the academic load.

This is a precious year as our butterflies emerge and begin to feebly test their wings. They are still unsure of themselves in many ways, but we have two more years to teach them to fly.

Notes:

The Critical Junior Year

Jeannette: It is heartbreaking when panicking parents call me late in their child's junior year or early in their senior year of high school needing help. The problem? Either the child has suddenly decided they want to apply to a competitive school or they have just realized that they are missing key subjects and/or necessary tests. This late in the game there is little I can do other than suggesting an extra year of high school or helping them lower their expectations for the type of college to which they will apply.

What Needs to Happen During the Jr. Year

There is no way around the fact that the junior year is a long haul. For students with their eye on competitive schools, this is the testing year in more ways than one. Remember that many competitive colleges require at least 2 SAT Subject tests and a few require 5 or 6. If you know where you want to go to college, check this out as a freshman and plan accordingly. My students try to take only one SAT Subject test per test date (there are 6 dates per year. Check out CollegeBoard.com), but take no more than two per test date.

> "For students with their eye on competitive schools, this is the testing year in more ways than one."

We have addressed testing in previous columns, but have not discussed the timeline. The sophomore year will ideally hold 1 AP class/test and 1 SAT Subject test.

Here's what the junior year test schedule looked like for one of my students:

Oct. 19	PSAT
Dec. 2	SAT
May 5	SAT re-take
15	AP Chemistry
17	AP Macro Economics
June 2	Chemistry SAT Subject test
Oct 2	Math Level 2 SAT Subject test

The summer after the junior year should be spent putting college applications together.

What Should NOT be Happening the Jr. Year

I have been helping students develop their leadership abilities and public speaking skills for over 25 years. I am a firm believer in the value of extracurricular or cocurricular activities, of work experience, of public service. However, a majority of homeschoolers put too much emphasis on these things (hoping for scholarships) to the detriment of cultivating their intellectual abilities. Too often I have seen high school juniors so involved in traveling ministries, in demanding internships, in challenging sports that they miss important coursework and/or college entrance tests or do not have time to prepare properly and therefore score well below their abilities.

We must remember that college is an academic exercise. If our children cannot perform in the classroom, they will not be successful at competitive colleges. SAT scores will usually determine the first cut in admissions offices. If your student scores within the range accepted by the college, the non-academic profile is considered. If they don't score well on the SAT, all the activities are for naught.

The answer? Try to maximize leadership opportunities as freshmen and sophomores. Use summers for leadership or traveling. If the only leadership/service opportunity is during the school year, you must make up course work over the summer (which happens only for very disciplined students). Better yet, push hard academically the freshman through junior years and travel or pursue internships as a senior or super senior year after your college applications are basically completed. This is not to say that you should ignore service and leadership activities, but hold them in a delicate balance with academics.

It is so easy in a homeschool situation to allow our children to spend inordinate amounts of time in the areas they excel and totally ignore the academic areas in which they struggle. To do so will cripple your children in many ways.

Stress Management

The schedule for this year is grueling, but a wise homeschool parent will help their student manage the stress. I bought my daughter a thick test prep book for each test that she wanted to take (there were 6 her junior year), but I also bought a hammock. When her eyes began to cross, I sent her outside with a good book to read, whether or not her assignments were finished. I would prepare tea for a needed afternoon break. I made sure she had time to exercise, time to study the Bible, and time to debrief on a daily basis. I helped her learn to more efficiently manage her leadership activities.

However, there are some things I do not allow during the junior year. I do not allow her to help me with the details of running our home (cooking, cleaning, laundry, caring for younger siblings, etc.) even though she dearly loves to do those things. She knows how to work and how to manage. This junior year is her year to test her abilities, to prepare herself for the college of her dreams. This year is my gift to her and to my grandchildren. She does pursue her leadership activities, but at a lower level than in years past. She has had to drop back to only 2 hours of music practice per day which is not ideal, but all her packed schedule will permit.

The junior year is arduous, but it is also magic. I watched both my children walk through the crucible and emerge on the other side as competent, confident adults. They came through the fire sure of their faith, sure of themselves, sure of their ability to make it in the world. And that, my friend, is why I homeschooled in the first place.

> **Austin:** Each family needs to determine what they are willing to sacrifice to meet educational goals. My sister and I were willing to spend our junior years, but no more, jumping through admissions hoops. We were willing to take 3 SAT Subject tests, 1-4 AP tests, and the SAT, but no more. If a school had unreasonable requirements (i.e. 5-6 SAT Subject tests), we rejected them. My junior year wasn't fun, but in addition to winning me a spot at my dream school, it taught me focus, time management, and the importance of delaying gratification. All of these things proved critical for me at Caltech and are certainly important in the real world.

Notes:

Senior Year: The Final Lap

Jeannette: One more year… one last time for the activities of childhood… one last chance to be a 24/7 role model for our children… it will never be the same again… if I don't say it now, chances are it won't ever get said… if I don't do it now, I may never have another chance. Though the senior year has plenty of "To Do" lists, you simply must take the time to cherish the moment. Trust me.

Final Testing

If we have planned well, all the college entrance testing will have been completed by the summer of the junior year. However, sometimes we get behind or we need to re-test. Be aware that the October test date is usually the last one accepted if your student applies Early Action to a college (applications usually due mid-Nov.). December is usually the last test date for Regular Action applications (usually due Jan. 1).

It is not a good idea for students to cram all three SAT Subject tests into this last test date or to take their SAT for the first time here. This is almost always a disaster! Plan well ahead so the senior year is not frantic.

The College Application Process

Ideally, college applications are completed the summer before the senior year, but most of us don't get everything finished by then. So, we have to lean heavily on the scheduling skills we learned the sophomore year and honed to perfection by the end of the junior year.

Using blank calendar pages, schedule in everything that has to be done:
- Final research on college options
- Attending college information sessions
- Scholarship applications
- Phone calls to admission offices for clarification on homeschool student applications or fine art requirements
- Essay writing
- Preparing the transcript
- Developing the school profile and transcript legend
- Writing the counselor letter
- Doing the research about each college for your teacher recommenders and giving them stamped, addressed envelopes for each college
- Filling out online applications for each college

- Filling out financial aid forms for each college
- Filling out scholarship applications for each college
- Submitting test scores (both SAT/SAT Subject tests and AP tests to each college)
- Recording music for fine art supplements or compiling artistic portfolios (if needed)
- Submitting the secondary school report
- Submitting the fine art supplement (if needed)
- Submitting the midyear school report
- Submitting the final school report

The list is truly daunting and most of it has to happen before January 1st. That is why it is so helpful to get a head start by beginning your work midsummer when colleges update their websites with the current applications, time lines, and essay topics.

Interviews

We also want to allow time for practicing college interviews. Some interviewers will meet you at a local coffee shop, some at a restaurant for dinner, some will come to your home. During Austin's senior year, we had just moved into an old farmhouse and were in the middle of remodeling when an interviewer called and insisted on conducting the interview in our home! So, be forewarned. These don't take up huge amounts of time, but must be planned in advance and rehearsed. See Austin's complete article about interviewing on page 102.

College Visits

Many people recommend a college tour to visit all the colleges you are interested in. We thought this was necessary and made the huge sacrifice to make the cross-country trip after my son's junior year. He even spent six weeks one summer at MIT and thought he knew the atmosphere of the school. He was shocked when he returned for a freshman preview weekend during the school year when the campus was crowded and the weather was gray and dismal. Even his visit to Caltech gave him a faulty image of the school. However, he made the decision to go there despite the initial negative impression he got of campus life. It has turned out to be a good fit for him.

We have come to the conclusion as a family that college visits can be postponed. If you are traveling through the area, by all means visit prospective campuses. If money is not an issue, the full-fledged college trip is fun and you may be able to eliminate some colleges from your list. But, if finances are tight, there is another way. If you are applying to a number of highly competitive colleges, realistically you will not be accepted at all of them. Therefore, it is possible to wait until after you receive acceptance letters to visit those particular schools or maybe even narrow it further and just visit your top choices to find the best fit. Be aware that a few top schools will actually pay for your plane ticket to visit them during admitted student weekends if you are financially needy. Don't plan on it, but know that the possibility exists.

The real scoop about campus is found during the overnight stay that is offered to pre-frosh (admitted students). Most schools have preview weekends where students can spend the night in the dorm, eat in the cafeteria, talk to others in their major, and really get a feel for the campus. However, be aware that a few days at the school will still not give you the whole picture of what life is like on that campus. There is just no reliable way to know a school until you live and study there.

> "If we have not captured their respect and their heart by this point, long lists of rules, furtive spying, and screeching admonitions over the phone will not help."

The final decision can be a difficult one for students that have a number of good choices. My daughter was agonizing over her top two schools when a wise professor told her, "Natalie, just turn off your brain and go with your gut." Sure enough, when she walked onto the campus that she eventually chose, she felt she had come home. Attending classes and visiting with students confirmed that her gut reaction was indeed right.

When doing early planning for the senior year, be forewarned that December will be spent in completing applications, which are due January 1 and April will be spent visiting colleges to make the final choice by May 1. Plan school accordingly.

Sr. Year Classes

It is important for your student to keep their grades up and to continue taking rigorous classes. Both my students continued taking difficult classes, but wanted to go deeper and thus chose to take fewer subjects. The load also seemed lighter because of the absence of all the extra testing. They also knew that they needed substantial time for all the college application activities as well as time to watch the sunsets and smell the roses before leaving home for good. The senior year for my kids was a bit of a respite before they moved on to pursue truly demanding degrees at top colleges.

Make Time to Celebrate

Because of the arduous nature of the last few years of high school, we looked for ways to celebrate. For example, after my daughter received her very last standardized test score and knew everything was fine, we built a bonfire to burn the huge pile of test prep books. She gleefully ripped pages out and flung them into the fire! Afterwards, we toasted marshmallows and made s'mores. We also took time to have daily rituals like afternoon tea or occasional celebrations like eating out with grandparents after her orchestra concerts. Extended family also need time for closure as they let go of young people headed off to change the world.

Inventory Skills

This year is your last chance to take inventory and see if there are any skills your children need that somehow got missed in the busyness of homeschooling. Does your son know the intricacies of stain removal and laundry techniques? What about ironing his shirts? If your child will take a car to college, do they know how to change a flat, check the tires for wear, or know the maintenance schedule of their vehicle? Are they financially astute and know how to pay bills, responsibly use credit cards, and deal with insurance issues? Does your daughter know how to protect herself in parking lots, airports, and public places? Do they know how to safeguard themselves from and treat various illnesses? These questions become very important if your children will be far from home. This is also the time to make sure that Mom and Dad know how to run the computer and DVD player!

Transitioning to College

If we have done our job well, by the end of their senior year our children should be ready to face the world squarely and make their own decisions. While my son has chosen to call me daily, it was not a requirement I placed on him. He has decided not to pursue recreational dating, but that was not by parental mandate. I find it troubling when parents monitor the Facebook and e-mail accounts of their adult children. We have had them in our presence constantly for the past 18-19 years. If we have not captured their respect and their heart by this point, long lists of rules, furtive spying, and screeching admonitions over the phone will not help. From infancy, I expected my children to be responsible and a mutual respect has formed that is daily easing this transition in our lives. I am thankful for the gentle changeover.

Notes:

building an academic profile

Turbo-charge Your High School Academics

Austin: In keeping with the spirit of my last column, let's ditch some more conventional wisdom. Many people seem to be of the opinion that homeschoolers should take as many outside classes as possible. Though there is nothing wrong with this and it may be the best use of available resources, my experiences have taught me another approach. Also, contrary to what some think, mothers CAN successfully guide their children (including sons) through high school.

What Colleges Want

Most top colleges have minimum high school academic requirements. Carefully check out the requirements of all your potential college choices. They generally want four years of math through calculus, four years of English, two to four years of a foreign language, four years of social studies, and four years of science to be competitive. They prefer that applicants take the most rigorous classes available.

Even if the student isn't planning to go to Yale or any college at all, that is no excuse to slack off in high school. You are shortchanging your kids if they leave home without a rigorous, substantial knowledge base including science, math, English, and history. They also need lots of practice in thinking and communicating well.

If your daughter just wants to get married and be a homeschool mom, great! Push her to get as much as she can from your homeschool, so she can teach her own someday. Since a homeschool mother will be the teacher and mentor of her kids she needs deep spiritual AND intellectual resources to draw on. I would be nothing if it weren't for my mom and her prodigious abilities, which she honed through college and graduate school.

Options

You have four options for completing course work. The classic homeschool way is self study, in which students learn subjects on their own or from parents. I even designed my own classes when I had a unique need. The other options, local colleges, homeschool co-ops, and distance learning, differ from each other in the details, but resemble institutional education (i.e. public or private school) methods in having an outside instructor. We term these "institutional methods."

Cost-Benefit Analysis
Any choice has costs and benefits. Academic decisions are no different. Instead of just picking what looks good, try applying rigorous cost-benefit analysis. Costs are fairly straightforward and can be evaluated in terms of monetary expense and time (time commitment and how much will it reduce flexibility). Benefits are more difficult, being either direct (i.e. quality of learning) or indirect (recommendations, help with college positioning efforts, etc.). We compare each option in terms of these parameters.

Concerning Dough
Education is expensive. Self-study usually wins the expense comparison hands down since it lacks tuition. For the institutional methods, there can be wide variation, but co-ops are generally the cheapest, followed by distance learning and local colleges. Ideally expense wouldn't be an issue, but for many homeschool families it is and they must make decisions accordingly.

Flexibility
For me, flexibility is one of the most important considerations. One of the greatest benefits of homeschooling is not being chained to a schedule. In my experience many opportunities only present themselves to those who have enough freedom to pursue them. If you're taking a full load online or at a college, chances are you will be quite limited. While the trade-off may be worth it, remember that inflexibility can limit your opportunities for growth in other areas and prevent you from doing things that might make you more competitive in the college admissions process.

Quality of Learning
Several things will affect how much a given student gets out of a particular class. The student's learning style needs to be accommodated by the style of instruction. For instance, I'm very independent and learn by reading and solving problems on my own schedule. As such, self-study is generally my ideal option, with text-based, asynchronous (meaning that there are no scheduled online meetings) distance learning coming in second. For students who are auditory learners, a more traditional classroom setting might look more attractive.

Before signing up for a class, research it. Does the teacher know the subject well? How much and what kind of interaction will you have with the teacher? An accessible instructor can make a class much more valuable than if the instructor is a talking head who hands out exams. Don't make any assumptions about the nature of a class.

Tangent Skills

Some classes teach you more just the declared subject matter. I took an excellent online biology course a few years ago with the intention of learning biology. However, in addition to knowledge of biology, I came away with greatly improved test taking and study skills, as well as the ability to write quick, test style essays. These "tangent skills" are side benefits whose usefulness transcends the course's subject matter. Whenever you are considering a particular option, especially if it is institutional, do a bit of investigation to see what kinds of tangent skills it might develop.

Validation

To do well in college admissions, you need some amount of outside validation. Validation generally comes in the form of standardized tests or class grades. For homeschoolers, standardized test scores are very important and grades (especially mom-assigned ones) are not weighted very heavily. An advantage of the institutional methods over self-study is that they give official grades, which have somewhat more credibility with admissions officers. However, due to grade inflation, top colleges don't generally assign much value to any grading scheme. The best thing to validate a course is take a standardized test, either AP, IB, or SAT Subject tests. Not all classes will prepare you well for a test, so research this as well.

> "Getting a letter of recommendation is both the most overvalued benefit of taking outside classes and the most frequently botched part of the application process."

Self-assigned grades for a class need to accurately reflect any associated standardized test scores. Don't put A+ for the subject on the transcript if the standardized test score for that subject is in the fortieth percentile. This will be a glaring red flag to admissions officers that you are not trustworthy. Get reasonable validation and be honest.

Recommendation Letters

Getting a letter of recommendation is both the most overvalued benefit of taking outside classes and the most frequently botched part of the application process. Recommendations are important, but you seldom need more than two and the recommender needs to be picked with great care. In most cases, a teacher from whom you have taken only one class is probably not the best recommender. Unless you know that a particular teacher will be an exceptional recommender and unless you will have the opportunity to really get to know them well, don't take the class just to get a recommendation.

Academic Curveballs

The ideas presented here can be useful to all kinds of students, not just those interested in top colleges. One thing parents need to know is that academically laid back students can suddenly blossom in high school and turn out to have great passion and aptitude for things academic. Even those who never showed interest in college at all can suddenly change their mind. If you haven't chosen a rigorous preparation program with the appropriate tests, it's easy to sink possibilities for college admission and deny the student an opportunity to fulfill his potential. By now, God has probably thrown you quite a few surprises through your kids. Be prepared, because the next one just might involve a bunch of college applications.

Notes:

PSAT/SAT/ACT and National Merit

Jeannette & Natalie: The Preliminary SAT®/National Merit Scholarship Qualifying Test is quite a long title for a little practice test that has up grown over the years into a significant recognition program. Not only is it the gateway for National Merit scholarships and other merit programs, but an outstanding score puts you on the radar screen of good colleges. Prepare to get overwhelmed with mail!

Contrary to popular belief, most National Merit Scholarships are not that substantial, being only $2,500 (either a one time award or spread over four years). The title only becomes financially significant when a college will match the award or offer big packages to National Merit Finalists/Scholars in the hopes of building an outstanding student body. One example is the University of Oklahoma in our home state, which recruits National Merit Finalists from all over the U.S. and offers close to a full ride if you list them as your top school with the National Merit Corporation.

If your student makes a certain score on the PSAT (the cut-off varies from state to state), he will be notified in September of the senior year if he is a Commended Scholar or a National Merit Semifinalist. Semifinalists continue in the program, sending in additional test scores, transcripts, a short letter of recommendation, and an essay. Most Semifinalists advance to Finalist standing, and about half of the Finalists become Scholars. But first, a good score on the PSAT.

What is on the Test?
The PSAT is approximately 2 ½ hours long and covers Critical Reading, Writing, and Math. The Math portion of the PSAT covers topics from your basic Algebra I course. These specific topics are: numbers and operations, algebra and basic functions, geometry, data analysis, statistics, and probability. The SAT will expound on these same topics, including information from Algebra II. So, plan on finishing up Algebra I by the spring of your sophomore year to allow concepts to gel before the test. If you can have Algebra II under your belt by this time as well, that can only make you more prepared and comfortable with the math.

The Critical Reading sections of the PSAT include two types of questions: sentence completion and passage-based reading. Sentence completion questions require the student to pick the best vocabulary word(s) to complete the sentence. The best preparation for this section comes from a lifetime of reading and learning vocabulary words and this is usually the least of a homeschooler's worries. The passage-based reading questions are your basic reading comprehension test: read a short piece of writing and answer questions about its meaning and perhaps the meaning of specific words in the context of the passage. This is fairly straightforward once a student has taken and analyzed a few practice tests.

The Writing section has three types of questions. The first requires students to improve sentences by choosing which answer makes the sentence grammatically correct. The second type has students identify grammatical errors in sentences by selecting which section of the sentence is incorrect. In the paragraph improvement section, students are asked to improve the readability of the paragraph by choosing different transitions or conclusions, correcting run-on sentences, combining sentence fragments, etc. To prepare for this, students should be comfortable with writing and editing. One should have an intuitive sense of grammar to be able to recognize and correct mistakes, but in these tests students are never required to name that split infinitive.

ACT or SAT
The junior year is filled with important standardized tests. The PSAT will be taken in October and will be followed shortly by the SAT or the ACT. There are also SAT Subject tests and AP tests. One of the time management decisions you will have to make is whether to take the SAT or the ACT or both. We recommend taking only the SAT.

To really maximize your time it is probably easiest to prepare for the PSAT by preparing for the SAT. Remember, the PSAT is the "practice" test for the SAT, so categories are the same and the questions are similar. This seems backward, but by studying for the SAT you've killed two birds with one stone.

There are also other reasons for taking the SAT instead of the ACT. First, it is considered by many admissions officers as a more desirable measure of a student's intellectual ability and hence, their ability to succeed in college. Secondly, it is accepted at any university coast to coast where the ACT seems to be more of a midwestern thing.

Exceptions to the Rule
While I do generally recommend the SAT, there are some exceptions. If your state, like Missouri, awards state scholarships based on ACT scores, and you plan to attend school in that state, go ahead and take the ACT. Otherwise, you could miss out on thousands of state scholarship dollars.

Some kids just score better on the ACT and feel it is a better representation of their abilities. To find out, visit www.kaptest.com/satactpractice and spend 90 minutes taking the SAT/ACT Combo Sample Test from Kaplan to help you determine which test makes you look best.

If you score significantly better on the ACT, by all means take it as many universities are accepting it as well. You need to do the research early to see what test your university of choice wants. If you take the ACT, do the optional writing section as well as it is often now required by colleges.

One downside of taking the SAT only is that some universities will require additional SAT Subject tests in science if you only take the SAT. My kids felt that it was worth taking the SAT Subject tests in a few science areas as they could prepare more easily for specific areas rather than deal with the preparation for and fatigue of a second huge test. If the ACT is your test, then you will just have to spend the extra time studying for both the PSAT and the ACT.

Test Prep Recommendations

As previously mentioned, we believe that the best use of time is to prepare for the SAT while preparing for the PSAT. You'll get an early start on the SAT and be over-prepared for the PSAT. Even though the PSAT is shorter and the questions are at a lower level, it is graded closer than the SAT. There is room for error on the SAT (you can miss a few questions and still get a perfect score), while the PSAT starts losing points with every mistake. There is also less time per question on the PSAT, so pacing is absolutely critical. This is why practicing is so important. Here are some places to start:

CollegeBoard: www.CollegeBoard.com provides some test information, sample questions, and, for a fee, test prep books, practice exams, and other resources. Sign up for a free daily SAT question to be emailed to you. Also, as the test maker, CollegeBoard provides the best practice tests to show what you need to work on. They sell a few old PSAT practice tests and also publish The Official SAT Study Guide ™, which includes 8 tests.

Kaplan: We have found that Kaplan's guides do an excellent job of showing students what to review, how to attack questions, and how to pace themselves during the test. They usually have practice tests that are very close to CollegeBoard's tests. They have independent PSAT and SAT guides.

These two are our favorites, but check out other resources, both online and at a bookstore and find what works best for your student.

Since the SAT (and therefore the PSAT) is a "Reasoning "Test," the best way to prepare is to get a few strategies from a good guide like Kaplan, then practice, practice, practice. Take 1-2 tests way out, just as soon as you have the requisite classes. Then, 4 months out, start taking practice tests in earnest. We recommend 8-10 practice tests taken once every few weeks to prepare. However, unless you take the time to carefully evaluate each test and find your weaknesses, you will not get the maximum benefit out of the practice runs.

When is it offered?

Students can take a practice run of the PSAT in their sophomore year. It is an unofficial score and colleges will never see it. My students were not ready mathematically, so we skipped that option. I was not willing to blow their confidence by taking it prematurely and failing. This is a judgment call by parents.

The actual PSAT (that counts) is taken in October of the junior year and must be taken at a local school. Hopefully, you have a good relationship with your local public school. If not, check out magnet schools, Christian schools, or college testing centers. Whatever venue you wind up with, double check the actual testing site. My very tall left-handed son was stuck in a tiny right-handed desk his first SAT try and the results were way below his ability. After that hard lesson, I became much more proactive in checking the testing site conditions (Is the room quiet? Will bells be going off? Will people be talking? Are the desks suitable?)

> "Academics count as 2/3 of the weight of your candidacy."

Unlike most standardized tests, you have one shot with the PSAT. No taking it over if you have a bad day. So, make it count!

Accommodating Students With Disabilities
The CollegeBoard is committed to ensuring that students with disabilities receive appropriate accommodations on its tests, and provides a broad range of accommodations to students who provide documentation of a disability. Check out http://professionals.CollegeBoard.com/testing/

Why Does Testing Matter?
Put simply, colleges view standardized test scores as one of the best indicators of academic potential. For homeschoolers, test scores assume even greater importance since Mommy-assigned grades are rather suspect. We must always remember that college is, first and foremost, an academic pursuit. Academics count as 2/3 of the weight of your candidacy. Given this scenario, it is wise to prepare yourself well academically and to prepare well for standardized tests. While the PSAT itself is eventually eclipsed by the SAT score in the eyes of college admissions officers, it is worth putting forth our best effort because of the many other doors it can open.

Notes:

Test Savvy

Austin: It's probably the most feared word in the English language, able to reduce normally confident students to convulsive wrecks in seconds. As you probably guessed, the word is "test." Like it or not, top colleges view test scores as good indicators of academic potential, so you must test well to be competitive.

What They're For
A number of factors will affect how you will perform in college, namely innate ability, work ethic, and preparation. To assess these, top colleges generally require you to submit one reasoning test (the SAT or ACT) and some combination of 2-3 SAT Subject tests. Be sure to check all colleges of interest, because testing requirements vary widely. Additional knowledge tests like the AP can be very helpful, but are not required. You can choose not to jump through the testing hoop, but that will severely limit your opportunities.

"Like it or not, top colleges view test scores as good indicators of academic potential, so you must test well to be competitive."

The CollegeBoard is Your Friend
The CollegeBoard website (www.CollegeBoard.com) provides detailed test information, registration services, and (AP and SAT) preparation books, practice exams, and other resources, free or for sale. CollegeBoard resources are generally to be preferred over those of other companies since the CollegeBoard actually designs the tests.

Reasoning Tests
Virtually all colleges require a reasoning test. Some will take the ACT, but the SAT Reasoning Test is always accepted and generally preferred, so I advise taking it. Take the ACT only if you score substantially better on it than on the SAT.

The SAT Reasoning Test doesn't require much specific knowledge. All you are required to know is basic math (including elementary topics from geometry, statistics, algebra, etc.) and some grammar, vocabulary, composition, writing and reading comprehension skills. This does not go beyond what is reasonably expected of high school juniors. If the student is proficient in these things and has prepared thoroughly, natural ability will largely determine his scores. Here, natural ability is an aggregate of being able to work under time pressure, recognize patterns, recall information, and solve problems quickly.

To score well, the student needs substantial preparation. There are lots of guides hawking supposed secrets for success, but don't spend much time on them. Pick a guide or two you like and learn the testing strategies, but use timed, realistic practice tests from the CollegeBoard as your primary preparation. This will help you get a feel for the test and find the strategies that work best for you. Taking practice tests increases scores up to the point of about 7-10 practice tests, then scores tend to level off.

Knowledge Tests

It takes more than quick thinking to do well at college. A student needs self-discipline, study skills, and a large general knowledge base. Knowledge tests are used to assess this. Though knowledge tests do involve reasoning, the emphasis is more on knowledge of a particular subject than on speed, as in the case of reasoning tests. We will examine the two most common types, SAT Subject tests and AP exams. These should be taken immediately after completing a class in the subject. Study with a good test prep guide (I like Kaplan) to make sure that you know what the test will cover, even if you have had a good class in the subject. Once again, the best preparation is taking practice tests, from the CollegeBoard when possible.

SAT Subject Tests

SAT Subject tests come in various subject categories. Offered six times a year, they are one hour long, multiple choice, and assume a previous high school level course in the subject. Preparation for the Subject tests should involve both study and as many practice tests as you can take under timed, realistic conditions.

AP

AP exams require more knowledge than SAT Subject tests and assume that the test taker has completed a college-level course in the subject. They are offered once a year on a specific date. AP exams are somewhat harder to self-study, because they contain considerable essay sections that require substantial preparation. However, it can be done with discipline. Note that some homeschool textbooks that call themselves AP level don't prepare you well for the test. Check what is required for the test and find additional materials to round out your knowledge.

The CollegeBoard has a number of useful AP resources. Particularly helpful are the released exams (real exams used in the past), which are available for several subjects. There are lots of online AP prep resources, so you'll need to do some research if you are interested in this option. The Apex Learning Exam Review was helpful to me and I had an excellent experience with one of the PA Homeschoolers online AP classes.

Being Honest

If you call something an AP class on your transcript, always take the test and base the final grade on the AP score. Depending on who you ask, a 5 is an A or A+, a 4 is a high B or a high C, a 3 is a passing C, and a two or below is a problem. Once you take a test, it is permanently on your record and will be sent to a college any time you send them any AP score. Don't call it an AP class unless you take the test, and don't take the test unless you are confident of scoring at least a 4 on it. If you are going to take an AP test, go ahead and take the related SAT Subject test. It makes life easier later on.

Test-taking Physiology

How you feel during a test can have great effect on your score. I've learned a few techniques to help you do your best.

Hard, physical exercise in the months of preparation leading up to the test can help maintain a healthy sleep pattern and keep your head clear so you can study more effectively. When you take practice tests, start them at about the time the real test will start.

At least several weeks before the test, determine how early you will need to get up in order to get ready and arrive at the test site on time. Be there about thirty minutes earlier than recommended so that you have some flex room in case something happens on the way. If possible, visit the testing site ahead of time to see if their facilities (namely desks) fit you.

Determine how much sleep you need to function optimally. At least two weeks out from the test, start going to bed and getting up at the same times you will be on testing day. Be sure that you get plenty of sleep the two nights before the test. The day before the test avoid studying or working very much at all. Take it easy and focus on calming down.

Diet is also important. Avoid sugar and caffeine leading up to the test. On test day, you might need a little caffeine to be alert. Try drinking a small cup of unsweetened tea. Another thing that will help you stay alert is to put a few drops of herbal peppermint oil on a handkerchief and breathe it periodically. The scent is very strong and will keep you awake, alert, and focused. I also studied with peppermint oil nearby to help with recall of the information.

Summing Up

Tests are a fact of life and especially important to homeschoolers. Play them to your advantage by knowing what's coming and being prepared.

Notes:

building an extracurricular profile

Choosing the Best High School Activities

Austin: First off, let's toss some conventional wisdom in the dumpster where it belongs. Most people pick activities based on what looks fun or what they think will look good on a résumé. My contention is that one should work backwards, first determining personal or career skills that need to be developed, and then finding (or better yet, creating) activities that will facilitate that development. In some cases a skill area is strong but needs to be extended, in others it is weak and needs to be brought up to par.

Top colleges are faced with huge numbers of strong applicants who have good test scores, solid academics, and many activities. To successfully compete, students need to prove that they are truly exceptional. This can be accomplished in any number of ways, such as by an outstanding commitment to an activity; by demonstrating unusual intellectual, artistic, or entrepreneurial ability; by overcoming a major setback, etc.

Admissions officers care about how applicants spend their time. Most of us spend it doing some combination of the following: academics, cocurricular activities (academic things outside of school like debate or science competitions), extracurricular activities (music, baseball, etc.), community service, and work experience. Basically, colleges are looking for excellence in 2-3 areas that fall within these categories.

Because of the flexibility homeschooling offers, we have unparalleled ability to train the exceptional people that top colleges want. But even more importantly, we can bring each student to their full potential by providing a unique environment in which to hone strengths and overcome weaknesses.

Stereotypes
In order to be effective in the application process, a student must understand himself: strengths, weaknesses, desires, and goals. That knowledge will help you carefully plan your activities. A good first step is to read *How To Get Into the Top Colleges* by Richard Montauk and Krista Klein, especially chapters 6-7, and fill out the Personal Profile Worksheets.

One important reason to "know thyself" is to understand what weaknesses the colleges will see you as potentially having. Any student will fit one or more basic stereotypes, each having probable strengths and weaknesses in the eyes of admissions staff. We differentiate between perceived weaknesses, which admissions officers think are likely based on your profile, and actual weaknesses, which may or may not be associated with your profile but could prove to be detrimental in college and in life.

My particular set of stereotypes involved being "rural," "homeschooled," and "academic." When these were considered as a sum, my perceived strengths revolved mainly around a strong work ethic and advanced academic ability. My perceived weaknesses were poor interpersonal and communications skills. True to form, I suffered acute shyness and a severe speech disorder. To combat these, my parents found a speech therapist to help me deal with my stuttering. To overcome the shyness, my mother started a public speaking class when I was 8 and helped me stay involved in speech and debate until the age of 18. Since I had difficulty interacting with people, my parents prompted (and sometimes pushed) me to practice interpersonal skills in Boy Scouts. We might have stopped when I mastered "getting along" with people, but mom and dad encouraged me to go further, to become a leader. My main training ground for this was involvement (both as a student and later as an administrator) in TeenPact Leadership Schools. By doing so, I was eventually able to overcome the deficits, even to the point of demonstrating that formerly weak areas had become strengths.

> "Contrary to popular belief, colleges are not looking for the "well-rounded" student who does everything."

Unfortunately, many homeschooled parents have difficulty confronting their children's shortcomings. Since most of us spend our time at home, it's easy just to ignore the problem, be it academic underachievement, social ineptness, a learning disability, poor manners, or the like. That may work while the student is at home, but one day they will have to face an unforgiving world. While you may be able to look past rough edges to see the good, most people won't. Help your child overcome his weaknesses. You aren't doing him any favors by ignoring them. Doing the right thing won't be easy because no one likes operating outside of their comfort zone. Expect some resistance, but persevere. If it weren't for my parents and their years (almost two decades) of persistence, I wouldn't have made it very far at all.

The Myth of Well-Roundedness

Contrary to popular belief, colleges are not looking for the "well-rounded" student who does everything (especially if he does not excel in anything). I've seen too many people run themselves and their families into the ground (and often into mediocrity) by frantically chasing activities in pursuit of a flawed ideal. It isn't worth it, to the student or their family. Pick a few activities and do them well.

> "Let's toss some conventional wisdom in the dumpster where it belongs. Most people pick activities based on what looks fun or what they think will look good on a résumé. My contention is that one should work backwards, first determining personal or career skills that need to be developed, and then finding (or, better yet, creating) activities that will facilitate that development."

The need for activities varies from case to case. Some students, if they have been spending their time in community service, working to support their family, or laboring on some other worthy endeavor, can get away with fewer traditional activities. Those with exceptional academic ability can count academics as one area of excellence so it usually suffices to have 1-2 other areas of involvement. For non-academics, it is advisable to be stellar in one area (be it art, music, business, etc.) as well as developing 1-2 secondary areas. Note that secondary activities need to be exercising a substantially different skill set. If you are an outstanding computer person who writes software and works as a technician, don't think that building databases for Habitat for Humanity will earn you extra points with MIT. Grab a hammer and build a house.

Life Preparation

I won't kid you. Skill development is a long, difficult process. If you are anything like me, you will sometimes wonder why you didn't take the easy route. The only thing that helps is to realize that the process of preparing for and applying to a top college isn't artificial or useful only for "getting in." It is the building of a person, a preparation for whatever life and work the student has been called to. Think of the college application as additional motivation for what needs to be done anyway.

On the other hand, don't idolize "getting into Harvard" or any other goal. Focus and hard work are good things, but don't lose perspective and forget what your ultimate goal should be (namely glorifying and serving God). It's easy to say "I'm doing the Lord's work" and promptly get so busy that you push Him right out of mind. I've made this mistake many times, and it always leads to being cut off from Divine strength and running on my own resources. It's a guaranteed recipe for unhappiness and failure. The first time I took the SAT, I obsessed about a high score. In spite of months of frantic work, test day wasn't pretty and the score wasn't nearly the one I had worked to get. When I relaxed and told God that I would accept whatever He gave, I took the test again and met my original goal. God has a way of breaking your idols, so don't create them in the first place.

Redeeming the Time

Time is a precious resource and careful management of it is critical. I hope this column will help your student get the most mileage out of his daily allotment by providing guidance in picking the activities to develop the skills needed for his calling. Life is short. Make it count.

Notes:

Building a College Résumé

Jeannette: The title to this article is actually a misnomer. It should really be "Building a Life and then Getting it Down on Paper." Of all the counseling I do, this particular area seems to be of the most concern for parents. "Are we doing enough? Are we doing the right activities? Are we impressive?"

We must keep in mind that all the activities should NOT be pursued for the purpose of getting into a great college (Okay, they help), but that should not be the real reason. We do these things to grow and develop, to push the limits on occasion, to find out that we are tougher than we thought. We do this to become all that we are, to find a new confidence and joy.

Why do I Need a Résumé?

As we are building a worthwhile life, we want to get it down accurately on paper. We will need a résumé to apply to college, to get a job, or to qualify for scholarships.

You must understand that competitive colleges and big name scholarships have thousands of applications each year. Everyone has incredible test scores, impressive transcripts, and outstanding résumés. In order for homeschoolers to compete, we have to be able to show that we have pursued excellence and have spent our life well. We do this by showing an exceptional commitment to an activity or cause, by excelling artistically or intellectually, or doing something out of the ordinary. Perhaps we have overcome some major obstacle.

Colleges aren't looking for cookie cutter kids, they are looking for students who have used their time well, who have made the most of the opportunities presented to them or who have created opportunities for themselves.

> "If you are an outstanding computer person who writes software and works as a technician, don't think that building databases for Habitat for Humanity will earn you extra points with MIT. Grab a hammer and build a house."

How do I Keep Track of all this Stuff?

In order to make a strong application, it is important that we learn how to keep track of the activities we do and the hours we spend doing them.

When my children were young, I kept records for them. In upper grade school and junior high, I began giving them more responsibility for keeping track of things. Each Friday I would remind them to record all their volunteer work and activities. In high school, kids should be on their own. I tried to make it easy for them in the beginning when I designed our weekly assignment sheet by recording weekly activities for them and letting them write down specific responsibilities or hours spent. I included prompts to get them to think through their week and write down special events. Eventually, they were on their own.

Now moms, it is tempting to do this for your children. Be forewarned that if you are still doing this for your high school children, they will be totally unable to cope with the scheduling demands of college.

> "Leadership is assuming responsibility for the outcome of a meeting, event, or project. It can be elected or assumed. Being a member of a group is not being a leader, being responsible to carry out something is."

Documenting a Life

You need to list specific activities and the hours spent each week. The student needs to record any leadership positions, committees, responsibilities, events organized, classes taught, numbers reached, as well as any special competitions and awards.

If they attend unique events, such as a week at camp or a conference, they need to keep track of the lectures, activities they participated in, and the time they spent doing each thing. Not only can this help with the résumé, it also helps you be able to document learning that can fold into a class for high school credit. You can separate out later what is volunteer service, what is work, what is school.

This may sound like a lot, but if done daily or weekly it only takes a few minutes. If you wait until your student's senior year and try to rely on memory, I guarantee you will forget many things and it could take you days of digging in order to reconstruct the minute details of her life.

Categories to Include
Once we have this documentation for each year, it is fairly straightforward to put together a résumé or fill out a college application.

As hard as it seems, your student's entire high school experience must be boiled down to one page. If someone with an MBA from Harvard Business School can do it in one page, so can you! You basically have 5 categories to report in:

> "In order for homeschoolers to compete, we have to be able to show that we have pursued excellence and have spent our life well."

Cocurricular activities - learning-oriented activities that take place outside of the classroom like debate or science competitions. Schools look at this category to determine intellectual vitality - whether your student loves to learn for the sake of learning.

Extracurricular activities - like sports, music, Boy Scouts. Schools want to see if your student is multidimensional or if they fit certain stereotypes. They will look to see if your student is a leader and visionary or just a passive part of the crowd.

Volunteer service hours - how many hours you have spent doing things for others. We don't count hours when we have been paid or when we are getting credit for school so we don't count our time twice.

Work experience - we need to show the years employed, name of the company, position/responsibilities, hours spent per week.

What Does Leadership Mean?
There seems to be a lot of confusion about the term "leadership." Not all kids are leaders. Not all leaders are charismatic. Very ordinary kids can be leaders when something is important to them. Basically, leadership is assuming responsibility for the outcome of a meeting, event, or project. It can be elected or assumed. Being a member of a group is not being a leader, being responsible to carry out something is.

What Words do I Use?
The words we choose to use in describing our involvement are crucial. Here are some of my favorites: founded, trained, taught, implemented, designed, facilitated, equipped, increased, promoted, organized, scheduled, one of _____ selected nationwide. If the word truthfully conveys what you did, use it!

Ordering Activities
We want to place the most important thing first, not list activities chronologically. List the overarching activity with total years of involvement on the first line, then list various events, leadership and awards that fall within that activity. This can be a painful experience as you must smoosh four years of great stuff into a few lines. Be brave. It can be done!

How you are trying to market the student will also affect the ordering. If you are trying to market an intellectual to MIT or Caltech, the academic information goes first. If you were marketing a would-be statesman to Harvard, you might put high-level leadership first.

If you thought the consolidation to one page was painful, just wait until we get to the college application.

Keeping Things in Perspective
The purpose of this column is to encourage you to do only those things that result in the greatest personal growth for your student and that truly benefit others, not to frantically grasp at anything that might impress a college admissions office. However, by using simple record-keeping and organizational techniques, we can then take these meaningful activities and show colleges how we have lived life.

Our ultimate purpose is to take our 5 talents or our 2 talents, invest them wisely and then be able to say, "Here, Lord! Here is your return for entrusting these talents to me." Oh, that we all may be able to hear Him say, "Well done, good and faithful servant."

Notes:

applying to college

How to Pick a College

Jeannette: Selecting a college to attend ranks among the most important decisions that your children will face in young adulthood. While many parents want to control this decision, I encourage you to enter it jointly with your child. It is their life and they ultimately have to live with the consequences of that choice. My children both made very different selections than I would have made at their age, but then I raised them to be much more mature and self-sufficient than I was. As homeschoolers, their education was far superior to mine and therefore prepared them for much more challenging fields and equipped them to compete at top schools.

Understanding Yourself

While it is true that you can survive anything for four years and youth makes you very resilient, I still counsel students to think about who they are and what they like before any serious college search begins. Is your student a "city kid" or a "country kid?" I don't mean where they were raised, but where their heart feels at home.

City kids thrill to the big city sounds of sirens, the throbbing pulse of the crowd, the excitement of countless museum exhibits. They might pick a campus in the heart of New York or Boston. All this noise and confusion will shut a country kid down. It feels threatening. Country kids need room to breath, green spaces, places of retreat. They might pick a campus that is either outside a city or is very spacious and private within a city.

Does weather affect your student? It certainly is a factor for some kids. One student, after visiting Boston, made the comment, "Everything was grey - the sky, the buildings, the people!" He needed sun and wisely chose southern California. He would have been miserable in Cambridge or Chicago. Some students choose to go somewhere very different from home just for experience and that's great, as long as they realize what they have to deal with. Be aware that most college visits are made when the weather is great. The same campus in the throes of winter is a very different place.

Does your student want people or privacy? Those extraverts with a host of friends might choose a large campus with thousands of incoming freshmen. There is always somebody new to meet and something exciting going on. There are countless clubs to join, but possibly few opportunities for meaningful research or relationships with professors. The chance of being taught by TAs (and not professors) is much higher here with class sizes numbering in the hundreds. Ironically, there is also the chance for anonymity on a large campus; no one knows your business unless you want them to.

If your student thrives on deep relationships with a few individuals and likes knowing everyone he meets on campus, a small school would be a better choice. Here administrators and professors know you by name and you get more personalized attention and opportunity for specialized projects. There will be fewer options for majors and a smaller selection of classes. The smallness is a cocoon for some and claustrophobic for others. You can't hide here, everyone knows you.

> "Be aware that if your student plans to go to graduate school at a top-ranked institution, chances are they will need to get a bachelors degree at a good mid-tier school or be an absolutely stellar, top-ranked student at a strong state school."

Even more important than the logistical and environmental issues is the deeply embedded personality of your student. Are they resilient? Can they bounce back from failure repeatedly? Are they flexible and able to live with (and love) people with very different values, morals, and beliefs than their own? Is your student tenacious? Can they hang on to their dreams despite opposition and obstacles? If your answer to any of these questions is "no," they are not ready for the challenge of a cold, hard, intellectual campus experience. You must search hard for the truly Christian campus that will give them time to mature.

Check your Field
It is easy to Google the top ranked schools in your field of interest to get the industry

take on various colleges. This will tell you which schools are considered powerhouses and command the attention of recruiters in particular fields. It gives us a place to begin our research.

> "Christian kids who are grounded and mature thrive in a top college environment. Students who are not mature start sliding fast at any college, including Christian."

While some students are fairly sure of their major, it is always wise to select a school that gives you room to move. It is also important to think about what else your student would like to pursue. For example, my daughter wanted an engineering major at a well-respected science school AND continue her violin study with master teachers. As a safety net, she also wanted a strong math and physics department should she decide to change majors. We had to find a school that offered all of the above (not an easy task). Finally, we needed schools with a history of generous financial aid, either need-based scholarships or merit scholarships.

As we began our search, we found some schools that offered a fabulous math department but a mediocre engineering department. For my student who could go either way, this was not a good choice. Some schools were engineering only, leaving no room to change majors. Some schools did not have engineering at all. Some schools had great science, but had limited opportunities for music or did not have good financial aid. This sifting and sorting process was the first of many steps.

Be aware that if your student plans to go to graduate school at a top-ranked institution, chances are they will need to get a bachelors degree at a good mid-tier school or be an absolutely stellar, top-ranked student at a strong state school.

Once you've narrowed the schools to those who have what you want, you must then carefully scrutinize each school.

What to Read
If you are considering a top or mid-tier school, I recommend starting with *Choosing the Right College: The Whole Truth About America's Top Schools* by Intercollegiate Studies Institute. Updated frequently, this huge book looks at America's top 100 schools and gives you a

perspective on campus life as well as statistics on admission, crime, cost, and student debt. They look at the outstanding professors on campus, core academic requirements, and whether the school offers a true Western civics core component. While ISI does tend to focus more on the liberal arts rather than the quantitative subjects, it is invaluable to get a feel for each campus. They report the overall scoop on speech codes, co-ed bathrooms, sensitivity requirements, alcohol and drug use, etc.

ISI also publishes *All American Colleges: Top Schools for Conservatives, Old-fashioned Liberals, and People of Faith*. This book has the same format, but lists ISI's favorite schools – usually small, liberal arts schools that do a good job with the Western canon. I also keep an eye on publications like *World* magazine which frequently reports on the academic freedom of colleges both Christian and secular.

Talk to Students/Alums
One of the most helpful things to do is to talk to alums and students in your major, particularly upperclassmen and those recently graduated. There can be vast differences between departments on a single campus.

New students are still enraptured with their newfound freedom and are still very positive, older alums are loyal to their core and have forgotten many things. Schools can also change drastically through the years. Upperclassmen and recent graduates can be bluntly honest about the good points and the shortcomings of their school. Questions to ask:

> *What is the best thing about this school?*
> *What is the worst thing about this school?*
> *Did it prepare you for your job?*
> *Would you choose it again?*
> *Are professors open-minded or do they have an agenda?*

Ask your department of interest who is recruiting their graduates. What grad schools have accepted their students? What are their strengths and weaknesses? How do they compare to similar departments at the other schools you are looking at?

The Campus Visit
Are there safety issues at this school? What is the neighborhood like around the campus? How many assaults occur yearly on campus (available in the ISI Guide)? Is public transportation safe? We found that students were much more honest about this than the administration. Another part of the safety issue is whether campus housing is guaranteed for 4 years. For schools that are surrounded by bad neighborhoods, this problem is magnified. Safety is an issue for any student, but particularly for females. Several schools that were

options for my 6'2" weightlifting son were not options for my willowy 5'6" daughter.
Is there an anti-Christian feel on campus? How strong is the campus Christian group (Campus Crusade, Navigators, InterVarsity)? Are there solid churches within walking distance (for the student who does not have a car)?

What kind of posters are up on bulletin boards and public places? Be aware that campus newspapers always attract the far-left and the obnoxious, so don't assume they represent the tone of the entire campus.

Are people pleasant? Are the dorms light and airy or filthy and oppressive? Are dorm suites or bathrooms co-ed? Are there many militant, combative activists around campus?

Apply to a Range of Schools
It is important that your student not set their heart on a single school, especially if it is a competitive school. Top schools can receive up to 29,000 applications for only 2,000 slots. For this reason, we must select a range of schools that they can be comfortable with - stretches, possibles, and safeties.

Don't be Afraid of the Top
My experience has proven that Christian kids who are grounded and mature thrive in a top college environment. Students who are not mature start sliding fast at any college, including Christian. Unfortunately, many Christian schools are that in name only and, because students feel "safe" going there, find their faith undermined by professors they think they can trust.

Students should not make the critical college choice because of the name of the school (Harvard) or the label it has (Christian), but on the school that offers them the atmosphere and academics they want. It has to be the right fit for them. It doesn't matter that it's not the right fit for someone else. There are fine Christian schools and there are horrible elite schools. But the reverse is also true.

Notes:

Selling Colleges on You

Austin: In this episode, we'll learn how to compress a normal-sized student into a few sheets of paper. Sort of. To do well in college admissions, you'll need to convey lots of information in limited space.

Test score and grades convey important but narrow information. Any top college could probably fill their entering class several times over with applicants whose scores and grades are equal to or better than yours, so you must show that there is something unique about you that sets you apart from those of similar academic credentials and makes you worthy of admission.

> "Think of the admissions process as Marketing 101. It just might be the most important class you will ever take."

Capturing the Elusive Self

When applying to college, the first thing you need to remember is that the admissions committee doesn't know you from Adam. Enlighten them by distilling the essence of yourself into a few main ideas and putting them on paper. It is impossible to talk about everything you've done or all the facets of who you are, so carefully choose only those things which communicate competence, leadership, growth, initiative, etc.

Who Are You?

The relevant features of who you are (for college application) fit in three categories: defining characteristics, personality descriptors, and background. You must distill 2-4 main talking points from each of the three categories.

Your defining characteristics, as I call them, sum up salient features of yourself and your goals. Articulating this isn't easy, but you should be able to come up some ideas that give a good snapshot of you, including major motivations, life and academic goals, career aspirations, etc.

By personality descriptors we don't mean things like "shy" or "quirky," but relevant characteristics like initiative, determination, intellectual curiosity, etc. By convincingly demonstrating desirable characteristics you can greatly improve your chances of admission.

The main points about your background could include important things that influenced you in the formative years, your family's philosophy of education, etc. Unusual circumstances, like growing up on an isolated farm or being a missionary kid in the South Pacific, can make you much more attractive to colleges so be sure to include them if they seem appropriate.

What Are You Doing Here?
You must also demonstrate that you have spent your time well. Do this by developing 2-4 main talking points each about work experiences, activities, and academics.

For work experience you should have one talking point about each job you have held in high school and what you learned from it. Unusual jobs, like working for a circus, being an auctioneer's assistant, or running your own business can be especially memorable for an admissions officer. However, almost anything will do as long as you can show that you did or learned something worthwhile.

Similarly, each of your major activities (be they extracurricular, cocurricular, or otherwise) needs to have a point and an explanation of what you learned from/contributed to the activity. With regard to activities, you must employ some bookkeeping in order to receive full credit for what you do. Carefully keep track of hours spent, especially community service hours, and the number of people reached, number of workshops taught or demonstrations given, etc. It is also important to know if your activities are on a local, state/regional, or national level. For example, most of my time in Boy Scouts counted as a local activity, my sister's participation in a state youth orchestra was a state/regional level activity, and attending the Research Science Institute was a national activity.

Admissions officers would rather see a few long term commitments than lots of short term ones. Additionally, a few serious activities are much easier to get across in an application. If you are in junior high or early high school, try to focus your energies on doing a few things well. You will probably get more from this personally as well as being more competitive for admission.

For academics, figure out the important academic milestones in high school and how they have shaped your development. Usually they should be successes, but failures may work if you can convincingly demonstrate that the failure taught you something important.

Building a Candidacy
Each point should illustrate something important about you and should fit into an overall portrait of you. As far as is possible, you need to make sure that your main talking points are communicated in the application, interviews, essays, and recommendations. In this process, I am NOT advocating that you construct an artificial persona. That is a bad idea and will probably result in you getting burned. The chances are that the admissions officers

will see right through the façade or that you will end up in an institution that isn't suited to you. A breach of honesty is serious and could have negative consequences for both you and other homeschooled applicants.

Colleges Have Wish Lists, Too

Once you understand your candidacy, you must learn to market it by understanding your prospective "customers." Your strategy will probably need to change a bit from school to school. Generally speaking, you won't want to completely change your strategy for each college. It is better to stick closely with your original marketing plan, but emphasize different aspects of your experience to be in keeping with what the school is looking for. Research college websites and admissions materials to determine what each college wants and how you fit into that ideal. They will all want the standard things like solid academics, but each school's philosophy will determine a set of characteristics it desires in students. This is best illustrated by a series of examples, which are a combination of others' observations and my own experience in working with each school.

MIT places great value on initiative and on the willingness to take risks. If you have single-handedly started an activity or built something that wasn't there before, emphasize it.

The University of Chicago seems to value a slightly artsy brand of intellectual curiosity. If you are a person of wide-ranging intellectual interests, like a prospective math major who wants to take advanced courses in Japanese language and culture, make sure that they know it.

Harvard seems less interested in what you do than in your motivations. During my admissions interview, my interviewer always followed up a question about academics or activities with a "Why did that interest you?" or "What is your motivation for pursuing that?" type question. Applicants to Harvard might profit by discussing what drives them.

The Big Picture

You will use the same talking points in all phases of the application: essays, interviews, letters of recommendation, and the application itself. It's worth your time to do this first step right.

Don't think of the marketing process as an annoyance that you just need to survive to get into college. Marketing is a very important skill, no matter where you go in life. Think of the admissions process as Marketing 101. It just might be the most important class you will ever take.

Notes:

The College Application

Jeannette: The complete college application is actually composed of many parts. The First Year Application includes: Essays, Letters of Recommendation, Secondary School Report (includes the Transcript and School Profile/Transcript Legend), Fine Art Portfolio (for music and fine art majors), the Financial Aid Application, the Mid-year School report, and the Final School report. It is imperative that you pay careful attention to each of these categories and their deadlines since homeschoolers are in the unique position of providing ALL the information the school will receive (with the exception of the teacher recommendation letters).

> "Eventually the Lord will give us the opportunity to share our faith. If we go in under the banners of a crusade decked out in Christian tee shirts and fish paraphernalia, chances are we'll never have the opportunity at all."

Be Careful with Details
College applications are almost always offered online, which is preferable to the old style paper application with lots of Whiteout covering our mistakes. We want a professional presentation and we increase our odds of success by using the online option. You will also often have the choice of filling out the school's own form or the Common Application. With the Common App, you can apply to multiple schools with one application. Some schools will request their own Common Application Supplement, but you still save time using this option. However, if you have a single school that is your top choice, it is wise to fill out their own application. This proves that you care enough to go the extra mile.

When you log on to the school website or the Common Application website (CommonApp.org) you will need to register with a username and password. Keep all this information together as you will be returning multiple times. If you apply to a number of colleges, it is easiest to write all the details down in one place: student's Social Security number and Common Application number, graduation date, GPA (weighted and unweighted), all test information for SAT, ACT, SAT Subject tests, AP tests, IB tests, (scores, dates taken).

As you are filling out the application, remember to ALWAYS FOLLOW INSTRUCTIONS! If you can't do it on a college application, they will assume you can't do it in a college class either. Word limits are a rule, not a suggestion.

Have a Strategy

Most people just start filling the application out, but the wise family will look over the entire document and strategize a plan of attack. You must cease being "mother" and become a master marketer. We must understand what each school values and adapt each application accordingly. Please do not misunderstand. We do not fabricate information and we do not present our student as someone they are not. We can, however, choose to present the information in a way the school understands and appreciates.

> "Choose to present the information in a way the school understands and appreciates."

Look carefully at each section to see what opportunities you are given to get all your information in front of them. In earlier columns we've mentioned "talking points," the most important parts of our candidacy that you want to present. Each college will give you opportunities in different places. Early in the application you will be given a form to list activities, academic honors, and academic year employment. Then there will short answer questions, and finally an essay or two. Look at the essay first. Which topic can you pick that will allow you to present your most important information or character trait? Then look at the short answer questions. Will they allow us to present the next important piece of information? Then use the forms to fill out numbers and show breadth.

To make this work, you need to be able to present your "talking points" in either bullet format for the forms, in a short answer question, or in a long essay. Each school will give you opportunities in different places and you must be able to present it well regardless of format. The short answer questions must be as carefully written as the long essay.

It is important that you form a cohesive presentation of your student's candidacy for all documents. In other words, if you list something in the college application, there should be back up information in the counselor letter, the letters of recommendation, etc. We don't tell the same story over and over, but the same story with different anecdotes, from different vantage points, from different audiences. The story may wax poetical in one letter to very factual on a form.

Part I

The rest of this column will deal with the First Year Application, or the first part of the Common Application. Aside from information like name, address, standardized test scores, and senior year classes, the first part of the application includes: Activities, Academic Honors, Work Experience, Short Answer Essays, Essays, and occasionally something extra.

How to Fill Out the Lists

The first big part of the application is the Activity Section. Here we must boil down the one-page résumé (outlined on page 69) and reduce it to approximately 6 lines - the very most important things about us. We list things in order of importance (which could change depending on the school) unless we are specifically asked to do it chronologically.

For Activities you will be asked to list the interest/activity and check a box for the grade when it happened (9,10,11,12, PG – postgraduate). The more checks the better. They like to see consistency over time - not serial joiners who have shallow commitment to multiple activities. They will then ask you approximate hours spent per week (this includes the activity itself, preparation time for the activity, and commute time), as well as how many weeks per year. They are basically looking at how you spend your time and what is important to you. Be careful though; make sure the hours you list per week in all the categories don't add up to more time than is available. This is a common mistake and makes you look dishonest.

It is also important to fill in all the boxes they give you. Break down some activities if needed. For example, instead of listing debate tournaments, awards, and debate leadership all together, you can list the competitive debate separately from the leadership element of your profile.

Finally, you will list positions held, honors or letters received in each activity. This is also the place to list your leadership - numbers of people reached, numbers of classes taught, etc. Always fill up the space allotted to you.

The secret of filling out these forms is to keep typing to see how much room you actually have. The little boxes on the form are horribly deceiving and make it appear you only have room for one or two words. Often you will find you can write a good-sized paragraph to describe the activity. To be successful in getting everything in, literally count the characters you have and keep trying until you can get the right fit. Use numbers instead of words, a hyphen, sensible abbreviations, whatever it takes. Also, be aware that many online form boxes these days can be "stretched" by dragging out the lower right corner, giving you lots of additional space. This is another reason to use an online format. Paper formats do not give you the extra space.

Academic Honors will give you room to list the honor, the grade in which it was awarded, and a description. Work Experience asks for the specific nature of the work, employer, approximate dates, and number of hours per week.

Personal Details to Share – or Not

Sometimes you will be given the opportunity to list favorite things like books, movies, websites, keepsakes, etc. This appears to be a no-brainer, but needs to be handled carefully. These unique questions give the college a window into your life that the rote forms do not. While you should be honest, you should also be cautious. Most colleges are still a bit suspicious of homeschoolers and we need to always keep that in the back of our minds. We never know what type of person our admissions officer is going to be and we risk coming off poorly if we ignore the fact that many do not see the world through our unique vantage point. Let me give you some examples.

One of my clients wanted to list a survival handbook as his favorite book. While it was innocent enough (he was a Boy Scout after all), put yourself in the shoes of the admissions officer. The assumption could have been that this kid was a gun-toting survivalist nut. However unfair such biases and profiling might be, realize that in these post-Virginia Tech days admissions officials are extra jumpy about such things.

You must also decide how you will handle your faith. Some people want to be all out there and make it the focus of their application (which is fine for a Christian school). There's nothing wrong with that at any school, but be aware that it will be a point of discrimination against you in a secular environment. When the Lord has called Christian kids into hard campuses, I have advised them to keep their application sanitized of Christian bywords. If your list of favorite things includes Christian music groups, Christian books, Christian movies, and keepsake crosses, they think they know exactly who you are and will probably decide that you would not be a good fit for an intellectual community.

My family sees it like this - we are missionaries in a hostile country. We have to move slowly, learning the language, understanding the culture, and being a true friend. Eventually the Lord will give us the opportunity to share our faith. If we go in under the banners of a crusade decked out in Christian tee shirts and fish paraphernalia, chances are we'll never have the opportunity at all.

Print Preview

After several weeks of careful editing, thoughtful analysis, and looking at our application through the eyes of our chosen college, it is ready to go. But first, ALWAYS do a print preview. This will show you exactly what the college admissions officer will hold in their hand. Go over it with a fine tooth comb. Let it sit overnight. Only hit the "Submit" button after every proofreader in the family has carefully reviewed it.

Notes:

Your College Admissions Essay

Austin: It's been a long, long day. A lone admissions officer is slumped over his desk, surveying a towering stack of applications with bloodshot eyes. He pulls your application from the stack and starts to read your essays…

The scenario above can have greatly different outcomes depending on how you filled the white space. For admissions officers, essays are probably the most memorable part of the application and are the best and most controllable channel for your talking points, which we discussed in "Selling Colleges on You" (page 78).

The main purpose of the essays is to give the admissions officers a better idea of the person behind the application, as well as to assess that person's writing abilities. Since writing ability will be mostly fixed at this point, it is my purpose to offer advice in writing the essays so as to best market the applicant by picking essay topics wisely, writing essays that give an accurate, intriguing picture of the applicant, using talking points, and polishing these essays into an effective final product. The essay writing process can be viewed as a sequence that alternates thinking, working, and revising, starting out at the most general level and moving gradually to specifics.

As in all phases of the application process, honesty is paramount. Though it is important to have assistance brainstorming and editing, do not have anyone write your essays for you. The admissions officers frequently compare writing assessment scores with the essays, so someone who is a poor writer and cheats on the essay will probably get caught and be rejected.

What the Essays Should Do
Since the main goal of an essay is to communicate relevant information about the applicant, essays should generally stay as personal as possible. Additionally, since you are limited on space, you should avoid listing your accomplishments. These things will appear on your transcript and in other parts of the application. The essay should communicate depth and context, not résumé factoids. When possible, the essays need to illustrate growth, background, motivation, and your contribution to society. A good essay will generally deal with a single incident or a small part of your experience. Don't try to cram everything in. This is your opportunity to be creative and show the unique things that set you apart from the rest of the applicants. This means that you need to keep the focus on you, not on another person or on an accomplishment itself. With this in mind, you're ready to pick essay topics.

Topics
Some colleges will give you a range of choices with respect to essay questions. You need to be sure that all important main ideas come across somewhere in the application, short

answers, recommendations, or essays. However, it is critical that you pick a question that will allow you to write an essay that is personal, while at the same time providing a framework for the activity lists and numbers found in other parts of the application.

Writing Materials
You should try to get essay writing material from your marketing plan/talking points, but these things might not be specific enough. If so, go back to the experiences that first inspired your talking points. When possible, reread your journals or look through photo albums. Find anecdotes and ideas to flesh out and back up the point you are trying to illustrate in the essay.

> "When possible, the essays need to illustrate growth, background, motivation, and your contribution to society."

Planning
Beginning the writing process without careful planning can result in wasted effort and disjointed work. Use your ideas to outline the essay, maybe writing out salient parts of it. Make sure the structure is tight and logical, that it "flows" and fits with your marketing plan and the rest of the application (including other essays, if any). Don't expect this to come together quickly. In my own experience, it can take days or weeks.

Rough Drafts
Working from your outlines, write out a rough draft. Don't be concerned about perfection or spelling at this point; just get the ideas down in a decently logical and structured fashion. Keep in mind that you might not stick exactly with your original outline. Writing projects tend to take on a life of their own. However, be sure to keep the essay within what is needed for your marketing plan. Once you have a rough draft, take a break, a few days even, before looking at it again.

Successive Drafts
The rough draft will require editing and rewriting - lots of it. Initial editing and revisions should be concerned with overall structure and making sure the requirements of the marketing plan are being met. As the structure becomes more refined, revisions need to focus on the dirty details - spelling, grammar, punctuation, and word choice. Through it all, make sure you are answering the question. It is possible to write a great essay that doesn't answer the question posed by the application, but this shows that you are unable to follow directions.

Though you don't want too many editors (as with cooks and soup, too many spoil it), it is good to have a person whose insight and writing ability you respect look over and comment on the essay in its various stages. Parents are often useful here, but you should also try to get the opinion of someone further removed.

> "A good piece of writing can serve you in many capacities. While one must be careful reusing essays, doing so can save you a LOT of effort if you do it intelligently."

Recycled Paper
A good piece of writing can serve you in many capacities. While one must be careful reusing essays, doing so can save you a LOT of effort if you do it intelligently. If your marketing strategy is different for two colleges, be careful of using an essay written for one college when applying to the other. In my case, I wrote the essays for my top choices first, taking lots of time and care with them. Since my marketing plan didn't change greatly from school to school, I was able to reuse a few key essays (entirely or in part) for many different college and scholarship essays as well as use sections for short answer questions. One advantage of this is that you can rely on writing that is carefully vetted and that you know to be good.

Concluding Remarks
The essay is where the admissions committee really gets to know you. Keep this in mind throughout the writing process. I highly recommend George Ehrenhaft's book *Writing a Successful College Application Essay*. In it he states, "…present your reader with a little something to remember you by, a gift - an idea to think about, a line to chuckle over, a memorable phrase or quotation… Send your readers off feeling good or laughing, weeping, angry, thoughtful, or thankful, but above all, glad that they stayed with your essay to the end."

His advice is sound. If you write from the heart, you just might reach theirs.

Notes:

Essays that Bring Home the Bacon

Jeannette: In typical high school student fashion, my daughter was discussing her preparation for the SAT essay with another friend who was also soon to take the test. While my daughter had been practicing diligently for the essay, her friend's lackadaisical attitude caught her off guard, "Oh, I don't need to practice that. I already know how to write essays!"

I'm afraid this young person could be in for quite a shock when the SAT scores come in. While your child may be a good writer, do not make the mistake of assuming that this skill will transfer to the many types of essays she will have to write to gain entrance into a competitive college. Let's take a look at the various types of essays necessary for the college bound student.

The College Application Essay
The classical essay is what most of us mean when we utter the word "essay." In contains an introduction, three to five points (one point per paragraph), and a conclusion that ties it all together. This is the type of essay your child will use in college application essays, although there are also short answer questions that should be as carefully written as the essay. If we have done our job, most homeschool children should be proficient at this by their junior year. What many people don't realize is that students can write a stunning essay and still miss the point - that admissions officers want to get to know the student through their essay

SAT Essay
The essay now required on the SAT test is still considered a classic essay, but is written with severe time limitations. Many great writers would not score well on this type essay given the time pressures, little time to think, and no chance at rewriting. In fact, your child will probably never have to write like this again in their life and many people question the legitimacy of this portion of the test. However, it is a requirement and we must do it well to be successful.

We have benefited greatly from the new offering from the Institute for Excellence in Writing's *High School Essay Intensive: SAT Preparation and College Application Essay Strategies*. Mr. Pudewa shares many success strategies such as thinking about who will be judging the essays - mainly English teachers and journalists. English teachers are impressed with quotes from literature. Journalists like to see history and current events mentioned. Both look for large vocabulary and smooth writing style. By becoming a "specialist" in a particular novel or author and a particular period of history, your student should have plenty of quotes and life lessons on which to base his essay. For example, my daughter loves the work of Jane

Austen and we have read all her novels aloud and discussed them. She is fascinated with World War II and is currently taking an AP Economics class. Those three areas have given her plenty of material to write about in all her SAT practice essays. Mr. Pudewa takes the mystery out of the SAT essay and gives many tips for success on his DVD.

AP Essays

Essays that accompany the Advanced Placement tests vary as much as the tests themselves and far too many people are unprepared for this section of these rigorous exams. My son was actually in the testing room with a group of public school students about to take the AP Biology test when one of them exclaimed, "You mean there are essays with this thing???" There is no excuse for that kind of ignorance.

Let's look a just a few of the AP tests and the types of essays they require. AP Biology is an exercise in memorization and the load is formidable. In this essay, you throw out the classical essay format and just write as fast as possible telling everything you know about the particular topic you are assigned. It's important to use the vocabulary you've learned all year and you can even draw pictures to illustrate a point.

AP Economics is much the same as AP Biology. The essay is not about form, but about getting everything you know down on paper about the particular question. In fact, this essay is more like a series of short answer questions and it helps the grader for you to label each part of the question and any sub points involved. It is important to draw graphs and use economic terms in your writing.

According to an official grader of the AP U.S. Government exam, format and length do not matter. You will be asked to answer a series of questions about a certain topic and are encouraged to label your answers to corresponding questions. In fact, you may write very succinctly if you answer the whole question and use the vocabulary they are looking for.

Practice, then Practice Some More!

No matter what type of essay your student will be writing, the most important thing to do is practice multiple times under timed conditions. Understand the rules up front as each type of essay is so different. Test prep books are available on every type of test and there is plenty of information available for free on CollegeBoard.com. These resources will give you the grading rubric for each type of essay. Grade your practice attempts honestly and find your weak spots. Liberally use the vocabulary specific to each discipline in your writing. Write neatly. If they can't read it, don't expect to score well. Some have suggested to write as large as possible as this makes the essay look longer!

And finally, you must remember that test scores, which include essays, will always be more important for homeschoolers than for other students. Because colleges have no way of intimately knowing our educational philosophy, the rigor of our classes, or our grading biases, they will rely heavily on standardized test results. It is important to take the time to study, practice a lot, and perform to the best of your ability on any essay you attempt.

Notes:

The Counselor Letter

Jeannette: The counselor letter was one of the most difficult things I did as my child's high school guidance counselor. Not physically hard, but emotionally draining. Perhaps more than anything else, it crystallized for me our homeschool journey. I relived all our ups and downs, our joys and heartbreaks, our successes and our failures.

I saw in my mind's eye the curly-headed little girl who lived life at a gallop with clothing askew grow up into a beautiful and composed young woman. I walked again the journey of helping a shy and awkward introvert who cried over Algebra II turn into a brilliant mathematician who is comfortable in any social situation.

Of course, I did not write about all of this, but it was a powerful framework as I began to tell the unique story of each of my children. I encourage you to take your time with this letter. I started the summer after the junior year and spent several months. Not only is it of critical importance for your child's admission possibilities, but it can also be an incredibly rewarding experience for you.

Design a School Letterhead
Some of my clients have hired professionals to design a letterhead for them and the results were fabulous. My students each created their own with our desktop publishing software and came up with a very suitable design. Whatever method you choose, I encourage you to make sure it is professional and use it any time your school contacts the university.

Our letterhead included the name of our school, address, phone, student name, birth date and common application number or social security number (different schools ask for different numbers. But whatever number they ask for, they want it on EVERY piece of paper you send them).

Introduction
I began each letter by introducing the student as a senior is our school. You must take off your "mom" hat and think like a counselor. I then described the student's learning style, using adjectives that showed how they would function in a classroom or on campus. Then I gave a brief summary of our school situation. In our case, we were in an extremely rural area with limited options. By making this fact clear, admissions officers would be more likely to understand our unconventional record.

Next up is a paragraph showing how our homeschool functions. Are you still the primary teacher or does your student take responsibility for their own learning in high school? Does the student take the most rigorous classes available to them?

The Body

I am often asked how long to make the letter. Don't worry about length. Just tell your story beautifully and the length will take care of itself. Just so you know, my letters have been from 2-3 pages. By the same token, your letters must not be rambles. They have a very specific purpose and you should never stray from that. They should, in concrete detail, embellish your student's talking points in a way that no other source can do.

> "As a homeschool mom, teacher, and counselor, you have a most unique vantage point. You have the privilege of showing growth over a lifetime, of telling the most complete story the college will get of this child."

While my daughter's application was able to cover the amount of time devoted to music, some numbers for activities, and a short essay about the joy she has found as a music teacher, I was able to tell the story of her combining her music and leadership ability to take complete responsibility for a huge fund-raising concert. I could paint a picture for the audience of how she juggled the many roles of fund-raiser, marketer, saleswoman, graphic designer, and emcee. I showed the admissions officer how she conducted herself in the boardroom and with local media tycoons.

Natalie was able to tell briefly about being an award winner at the national NCFCA Tournament. Since there wasn't room on another part of the application, I got to tell the "rest of the story." Our family moved back to Oklahoma and shortly thereafter went through a financial crisis so severe that she could no longer travel to tournaments. Out of that devastation, she and a friend created a national online debate network. Like a phoenix rising from the ashes, she took a personal tragedy and built an organization that blessed many others.

I am careful to objectively show how my students compare to others their age, how they are unique. I am not afraid to discuss weaknesses and how they have been overcome. In fact, if your letter is completely positive, it can backfire. You can come off as totally unobjective, which is what they expected from a homeschool mom. Just be careful of being negative or whiny.

Finding the Right Conclusion

The final wrap-up is very important. It must be powerful. It must be persuasive. It must be honest. Perhaps it would help to see how I ended the letters for my children.

Austin: There are many gifted students who have had every advantage and opportunity. This has not been the case for Austin. Not only has he spent the majority of his life on an extremely rural farm and ranch, making special classes and tutors impossible, but our family has been financially unable to provide him with traditional experiences. For several years, Austin worked 10-20 hours a week doing construction work to help support our family. This was on top of farm chores and other odd jobs. While this was a very difficult time, it produced a young man with an incredible work ethic who manages his time well and is grateful now to have 8-10 hours a day in which to study.

Austin is an unusual mix of intense scientist, runner, policy analyst, comedian, political aficionado, backpacker, social/technological trend observer, avid reader, and compassionate friend. As a parent/teacher, it has been a challenge to deal with his intense nature, but after years of helping him sand off the rough edges, I can honestly say I enjoy the young man who now towers over me. He has chosen to live intentionally, to confront his weaknesses, and to build on his strengths. He is now comfortable with himself and with others.

Natalie: I have been involved with many high school students over the years, most of which fit fairly comfortably into certain categories, but I have to say that Natalie defies classification. She is equally fascinated by untangling the multiple voices of a Bach violin fugue and by analyzing the molecular signaling processes in slime mold. She loves Jane Austen and is a connoisseur of high tea, yet gets an adrenaline rush over calculus problems. She delights in performing for crowds in a beautiful long ball gown and then, the next morning, pulls on her work boots to care for the 1,000 pound steers in her feedlot. She is a leader who listens before she talks, an efficient administrator who is a gentle encourager, a personality who is strong willed, yet chooses to pay attention to those with greater experience. I admire her very much.

You Can Do It

As a homeschool mom, teacher, and counselor, you have a most unique vantage point. You have the privilege of showing growth over a lifetime, of telling the most complete story the college will get of this child. It must be bluntly honest without being negative. It must be compelling without being sappy. It's a big job, but one that brought me much joy.

Notes:

Getting Great College Recommendations

Austin: Most colleges won't just take a mother's word that her children are wonderful. Homeschoolers need an objective, third party appraisal of their academic and personal abilities. Fortunately, the letters of recommendation that most top colleges require allow for just that.

A Special Role
Letters of recommendation serve as a special "window" into the applicant for the admissions committee. They are more objective than essays but more personal than grades and test scores. A good recommendation helps to show who the person really is by sharing specific anecdotes about and observations on the applicant so as to support the applicant's marketing strategy. Recommendations are critically important and can destroy a candidacy if they are not written carefully (even if positive in tone).

The Big Picture
The recommendation letters need to fit the overall marketing plan and work together, each addressing a different aspect of your candidacy. For each college, I generally submitted three letters of recommendation: one from my mom (the counselor letter), one from my science mentor, and one from my speech teacher.

My mom's letter discussed the challenges I had overcome, my leadership skills, and my growth as an individual over a lifetime. I asked my science mentor to detail my strengths: scientific and intellectual ability. My speech coach addressed my interpersonal skills and public speaking ability. Basically, she showed that perceived weakness in interpersonal skills did not apply in my case. She was able to demonstrate that I cared about other people, worked well in a group, and had a sense of humor.

Picking a Recommender
There are many factors to consider when picking a recommender and it must be done carefully. Start thinking early because you need to request recommendations at least two months before the letter is due in order to give recommenders plenty of time. Colleges usually have specific requirements, like one recommendation from a science teacher and one from a humanities or social sciences teacher. The recommender needs to be an adult who has taught or mentored you, who genuinely likes you, who wants to see you succeed, and who has the time and skill to write a good letter. Ideally, the person should have had many points of contact with you (some in the 11th or 12th grade) and a vested interest in your success. Just because you were a student in their class does not mean they care about you or know you well enough to write a great letter.

Any time you ask someone to be a recommender be sure to give them the option of saying no. This is polite and wise on your part since you don't want a letter from someone who doesn't want to write it.

Preparation

Once the person agrees to be a recommender, you need to prepare some documents to make their job as easy as possible. First, determine what you need from the recommender. To do this, you must understand your marketing plan for and application to the particular school, including what you will be able to address where. Lists of your accomplishments and evidence of being a "good student" will appear in the written application, so a recommendation that doesn't say much other than that you are a good student doesn't accomplish much.

In light of what has not been covered in the application, or what needs to be elaborated on by a third party, compile a very specific list of areas (like academic ability, personal traits, background elements, etc.) that need to be addressed and include that list in a letter to the recommender. Ask them if they feel comfortable addressing these areas. Also give them a copy of the college's recommender form (usually a part of the application) as well as specific things that particular college wants. You can also give them examples of a good and bad recommendation letter, your transcript, and résumé.

I used the same recommenders for all the colleges I applied to. This could have meant a great deal of work for them, but because I did the research for them and detailed what each specific college was looking for, they were able to address all the colleges' concerns with one carefully written letter.

The Counselor Letter

Most colleges also ask for a letter from the student's high school counselor. This is a good deal for homeschoolers, since one of the parents will write it. This allows you to more effectively communicate the student's candidacy, as the counselor letter can fill in details about the student that might not fit into other parts of the application.

I can't stress enough that the letter, like every other aspect of the application, must be truthful. It is a moral imperative to be honest, even if it weren't for the fact that admissions officers usually see through smoke screens. Don't be afraid to deal with weaknesses and failures, as long as you can demonstrate that you have risen above them. In fact, my mom was brutally honest about my early shortcomings (which fit in the typical stereotype an admissions officer would have had of me). However, I feel her well-written letter gave me an edge on the competition because she laid to rest any fears they would have had about my ability to fit into a highly structured, fast-paced environment and to interact well with other students.

Remember to Say Thank You

As with other parts of the application, it is important to express appreciation. Thank you notes to the recommender are a must and serve a practical purpose. Mail them shortly before the due date as a subtle reminder. Because I asked so much of my recommenders, I also gave them a small gift when the process was finished.

Keeping Track of Details

Application details can become overwhelming but there are ways to manage them. It is very helpful to create grids to keep track of the details. For example, we made a chart with the colleges I applied to down the left side of the page. Across the top, we made columns where we listed each piece of information that had to be sent to the college:

- Part I of the Application
- Part II of the Application
- School Profile and Transcript Legend
- School Report/Counselor Letter
- Humanities Teacher Recommendation
- Science/Math Teacher Recommendation
- Midyear Report
- Financial Aid Information
- AP test results
- CollegeBoard test results

As each piece of the application was mailed (or electronically submitted), I wrote the date in the box (i.e. MIT, Part I, 9-27-04). When the information was received by the college, I used a yellow highlighter pen to signify that it had arrived. A quick glance at the chart let us know what steps were finished and what was left to do.

I also learned that the postal service loses things. Do not mail important documents. I recommend setting up a FedEx account online so you can easily print shipping labels and track your documents to ensure that they get to the college. Use FedEx for all important documents. In fact, you just as well go ahead and purchase a large box of 9"X12" envelopes.

To make it easy for your recommenders, print shipping labels with the recommender's return address and give the labeled envelope to the recommender to ship the letter. This minimizes inconvenience and cost for the recommender. It also allows you to check when the letter is mailed and received.

Conclusion

Since homeschoolers have great ability to cultivate long-term relationships with mentors, we have the potential to do very well in terms of letters of recommendation. This is an area where solid character, competence, and long-term commitment can be proven and will yield large dividends.

Notes:

College Interviews

Austin: I confess. Interviews are not my natural strength and my first practice interview with an attorney was an unqualified disaster. However, I improved with practice and (surprisingly) enjoyed all of my actual college interviews.

Colleges use interviews to fill out their picture of the applicant and to gauge things like maturity, personality, and interpersonal ability. While much of the interview depends on factors beyond your control such as the interviewer and the deeper-seated aspects of your person, you can greatly improve how you "come off" in an interview by preparing carefully.

Talking Points

The interview is part of your overall positioning and marketing effort, so you should have your talking points in mind and ready to communicate. As with other aspects of the marketing plan, it needs to be customized somewhat to each school so as to emphasize those qualities the school wants. You may even want to write down your points. Don't memorize them to recite (this sounds canned) but be familiar enough with them that you know what to say and are comfortable saying it.

> "The interview is part of your overall positioning and marketing effort, so you should have your talking points in mind and ready to communicate."

In any interview, it is unlikely that you will cover everything. Therefore, pick out the 3-5 most important points that demonstrate something unique about you. These are the things that you want the interviewer to know for certain before the interview is over. Find a way to get them in!

Preparation

Few people are naturally good interviewers. Most of us need lots of practice to perform well. Start practicing with your parents. Move on to family acquaintances (especially lawyers) and ask them to be really tough on you and to try and trip you up. Videotape yourself for post-interview analysis. If you have friends who are also preparing for college interviews, try interviewing each other. This will help you spot common mistakes. To make the interview more realistic, prepare a list of common questions for the interviewer to use as a baseline.

Appearance and Demeanor

While appearance alone won't determine the outcome of the interview, it can help or hinder you. Above all, avoid sloppiness. This communicates carelessness and lack of interest in the college. Appropriate interview dress ranges from business casual to suit and tie (or the equivalent for ladies). While you will have to determine what works for a given situation, I would encourage you to lean toward the formal side of the scale. You can't hurt yourself by doing this, and doing the opposite runs the chance of offending some interviewers (especially older alumni). Young women should take pains to be modest.

In demeanor be mature and respectful, neither excessively nervous nor cocky. Contrary to popular belief, its okay to be a little nervous during an interview, provided that does not interfere with your answering questions intelligently and with some semblance of confidence. For detailed interview advice, the best book I know is *How to Get into the Top Colleges* by Richard Montauk and Krista Klein.

Questions for the Interviewer

The interview is not a one way street. Part of the idea is to learn about the college from the interviewer. Even if you think you know everything you need, it is imperative to have at least 3-5 questions for the interviewer about the college. It is important that you know the school well before interviewing in order to ask intelligent questions. This communicates interest in the school, which is something they desire.

Note that these should not be questions that you could easily answer by checking admissions materials. Most of your questions should require the interviewer's opinion. For example, you could ask, "What do you think sets the school apart from its competitors?"

Knowing your Audience

Generally, you will be interviewed either by an admissions officer, an alum, or a current student of the school. These types of interviewers are different from each other and there are things you should keep in mind when dealing with each of them. Always take your résumé and transcript to give to the interviewer at the beginning.

Admissions Officers

Admissions officers are the most professional and generally the best kind of interviewer. They have more access to your file than any other type of interviewer and will thus be better informed about your candidacy. They usually like teenagers and are good sources of information about the school. They will likely be present in admissions committee meetings when you are discussed and often become powerful advocates on your behalf.

Alumni Interviewers

Though not necessarily the most professional interviewers, alumni are often the most amiable and the easiest to talk to, especially if they are older. That was my experience, though I do know of some exceptions.

Be prepared for a home visit by an alum interviewer. In some regions without many applicants, an alum might have only a few students to interview and will want to come to your house and meet your parents. You may have to communicate more to them, since they may have not been given any information about you.

The downside of interviews with alums is that they are not the best sources of information on the current state of the school. Your questions for them should concern their experiences at the school, "How well did Princeton prepare you for your career?"

Student Interviewers
Though they may seem less intimidating because of their closeness in age to you, student interviewers present special challenges. Of the three types, student interviewers tend to be the least mature and, in my experience, the most likely to chase rabbit trails in an interview. Student interviewers are more likely to be threatened by you and more likely to show off their knowledge by trapping you with obtuse questions. This is not to paint them all with the same brush, but these are tendencies you need to be aware of so that you don't get taken by surprise. It is crucial that you know how to keep control of the interview and be winsome and humble in doing so. On the upside, student interviewers are the best sources of student perspectives on college life.

After the Interview
Don't assume the interview occurs only in the interviewer's private office. Consider everyone a potential interviewer from the moment you enter the building until you leave and treat everyone with courtesy.

Immediately after the interview, write the interviewer a thank you note (get a business card for their address and correct name spelling). It is also critical that you take time to think back over the interview and write down what questions were asked, what your responses were, which parts of the interview went well and how you could have answered better. This will help you improve for the next interview.

Conclusion
A successful interview is one in which you have winsomely presented what makes you unique. If you have a good interviewer and are well prepared, this should be fairly straightforward. In other cases the interview may wander off track and so you must know how to gently steer the interview back around to what you need to focus on.

Don't approach interviews with foreboding. If you have prepared, they can often be enjoyable experiences. This is one of the few time in life someone will ask you to talk about yourself, so make the most of it!

Notes:

7 once you get there

How Dangerous is College?

Austin: Hopefully my columns to date have given you some ideas for choosing and applying to colleges. A logical next step is to fill you in on what it's actually like when you get there. To that end, I have interviewed a few of my pals from around the country - currently at places like MIT, Harvard, the University of Chicago, the University of Denver, and the California Institute of Technology - to give you an idea of what the collegiate "marketplace of ideas" is really like.

Academics and the Rest of Life

I've spent some of the previous columns detailing the academic and career benefits of attending a top college, so I won't repeat much. Suffice to say that there are lots of opportunities at these institutions, including first-rate instruction and unparalleled opportunities for internships, summer jobs, and research. In many cases, simply attending a particular institution gives instant credibility when it comes to applying for jobs or academic programs. Deserved or not, reputation is a powerful thing.

Almost as important is what one can gain from other students. Much of what I have learned at college so far, I learned from my peers. Every one of them are very academically talented and many of them arrived as freshmen already with near-expert knowledge of particular fields. Watching bright minds in action is an educational experience in itself.

However, there are many social benefits as well. A friend of mine at Caltech once remarked, "What makes this school so great is that absolutely everyone, down to the slacker who wastes most of his life in computer games, has a sparkle of life, a sense of humor, and a story to tell." College is one of the few times in life that exceptional students will be surrounded by peers who understand them and can challenge them intellectually.

Faith, Freedom, and Politics

Christians, though definitely a minority on most campuses, are far from scarce and in some cases appear to be on the rise, especially at science and engineering universities, according to my MIT contact. There is some hostility towards people of faith in modern higher education, but it is not always the rule. Mary, a friend studying liberal arts at the University of Chicago, recounted an experience from her freshman year, "I was in a philosophy class, working with several other students. One of them started saying ridiculous, hurtful things about Christianity. It didn't last long, however. Several other students, none of whom were religious, took him to task and shut him down."

> "If a Christian college provides the education you need, by all means go to it. But never think of it as spiritual daycare for young adults."

I can't speak for all campuses, but I've found the Christian community at Caltech to be far ahead of just about all other Christian groups of the same age range in terms of spiritual maturity. In fact, one young woman I know attends meetings of the Caltech Christian Fellowship instead of the equivalent group at her nearby Christian college. She said, "I tend to spend a lot of time with this group. They are more serious about their faith than people back at my school."

Christians and conservatives are no silent minority. At Harvard, one of the more notoriously liberal Ivies, the political left does not hold any monopoly on activism. My friend at Harvard, whom I will call Heather, is also a liberal arts major. She said, "It's definitely a marketplace... The three most verbal, active campus groups seem to be the gay/lesbian association, the living wage/pro-immigration crowd, and the campus pro-life fellowship. I haven't seen any trace of a pro-abortion group... The campus Democrats are definitely more numerous than the Republicans, but the Republicans are more energetic."

Problems that Can Be Avoided
It is important to keep the dangers of college in mind; however, the common stereotype of the bullying, atheist professor ridiculing and corrupting Christian students in his class is the exception. Jennifer, a freshman at the University of Denver, said, "I've heard of one or two professors like that, but I've never had one in a class. The professors I've dealt with so far are some of the most amazing, brilliant people I know. They're very accessible and willing to talk about politics, theology, or most anything. While generally somewhat left of center, they are fair and open-minded, creating an atmosphere in which you can express any position that you are able to articulate and defend."

The closest thing I got to a complaint was from Mary, who mentioned that one of her biology professors tended to be a bit sarcastic towards creationists. "But," she said, "he was kind of that way toward everyone, and always in a good-humored way. Additionally, I was quite open about disagreeing with him in class and in some of my papers, and my grade didn't suffer for it."

There are real loonies out there, but I think you'll find that they tend to isolate themselves at certain schools and into fairly predictable academic disciplines, and are therefore possible to avoid. Generally, the wackiness occurs in less quantitative, academically lightweight disciplines like education, ethnic/gender studies, religious studies, and the like. Math, computer science, engineering, the hard sciences, and business tend to be apolitical or at least quite moderate. Government/political science, history, and literature vary a lot by school as to the degree of political correctness, so that has to be checked on a case-by-case basis. I highly recommend the ISI Guides *Choosing the Right College: The Whole Truth About America's Top Schools* and *All-American Colleges: Top Schools for Conservatives, Old-Fashioned Liberals, and People of Faith*. Basically, if you do your research before you apply to schools and ask around about specific instructors before taking their classes, you can usually avoid trouble. However, be prepared to drop a class if necessary.

> "I chose a top-tier institution because the academy is probably the most important marketplace of ideas on earth. It is the place where movers and shakers are made. It is important that the Christian faith and life be on display with all the other philosophies of our age, so that others may see the truth in it."

Christian parents, in my experience, tend to work overtime worrying about the amount of peer pressure their kids will be under in college. I can't speak for all cases, but seldom have

I observed students to be strongly pressured to do something against their beliefs. Mary observed that, "If people know what your convictions are, like not drinking or practicing abstinence until marriage, they won't try to talk you into doing something contrary and will generally respect you for what you are." Sending a student to college with their guard up about this kind of situation is kind of like building a tornado shelter in earthquake-prone California. Sure, it might be useful once in a great while, but you're taking a risk if focusing on imagined perils causes you to ignore real ones. Jennifer stated, "I'm of the opinion that most apologetics-oriented ministries do students a disservice by portraying college as a big, hostile battlefield. There are threats and problems, but they're usually rather covert."

Matters of Real Concern
External circumstances can certainly influence behavior, but what I have found is that people stand or fall based on what is within – external pressures can only accomplish so much, for good or ill. The main danger to the Christian college student is losing their deliberateness and getting sloppy and inattentive when it comes to their relationship with Christ and with fellow Christians. A student's first priority should be to spend time in prayer and scripture, and their next should be to plug into a solid Christian community on or near campus. In my experience, this needs to happen quickly, or it won't happen at all. Research for this can start before departing for school. Not just any Christian group will be suitable for the purpose. It needs to be a group that knows the student and can keep them accountable. It needs to contain people more mature in the faith who have the time and inclination to act as mentors. For this reason, a local church can often be preferable to on-campus groups, which can sometimes be just glorified youth groups with questionable maturity. A friend of mine, who now works as a physicist said, "If I had college to do over again, I would have invested more time in my local church than in the campus Christian group."

Some parents make the mistake of thinking that sending their children to a safe college environment will protect them. What they don't realize is that there is no such thing as a safe place. Don't think that an institution with the label "Christian" on it is safe from those who would try to undermine a student's faith. Even without external prompting, what's inside will manifest eventually. I know of homeschoolers that went off to Christian colleges at which the "wrong crowd" was pretty hard to find but they managed to find it anyway. If a Christian college provides the education you need, by all means go to it. But never think of it as spiritual daycare for young adults.

Trouble won't usually come looking for your child, but it is always there if they are looking for it. Like an opportunistic infection, it generally only gets those who are weak and floundering to begin with. By ourselves we are not strong enough, but our Father is there to support and strengthen if we will only stay close to Him. Your prayers and continual communication (family cell phone plans can help a lot) with your student can help keep them centered and ensure that any adversity that comes along will only make him tougher.

Parents have to come to grips with the fact that they no longer have the ability to control the behavior of their offspring when they reach young adulthood. If they are not strong enough to resist the temptation and antagonism of a secular college, they probably won't be safe in a Christian college, either. Neither will they be safe in a job down the street from your home. It's time to fly, or to fall. If you've done your job, all that's left to do is pray for them.

Stuff to Put Up With

Perhaps more pervasive than things that might lead student astray are things that disrupt peace of mind. Drunkenness, obscenity, vulgarity, and the like are facts of life in higher education and a student will have to learn to ignore it and get on with life. However, most students are fairly reasonable and, "something that really, really outrages you will probably outrage most of them also," according to Mary.

Choice of living quarters and roommates can be very important. On campuses where there is any freedom of choice in housing, dorms generally get definite personalities, which can work either with or against the student. For instance, there is often at least one "party dorm" on each campus, where noise and other downsides of college life concentrate. Do your housing homework ahead of time — it can save you a lot of headaches.

Just as important are roommate issues. Most of the college horror stories I've heard concern "roommate incidents." If you have any choice in the matter of roommates, pick carefully and don't make the mistake of thinking that a good friend will necessarily make a good roommate. It was once remarked that, "Two people can be good friends, or roommates, but usually not both at the same time." If you are more introverted, as I am, you might benefit greatly from a private room, if one is available.

Parting Thoughts

Hopefully you now have a better idea what life at college is really like. There are problems, but I think you'll find that, if your student is mature (spiritually, intellectually, and emotionally), picks his instructors carefully, and remains centered, the experience will be overwhelmingly rewarding. But for me, the issue is much bigger than my personal benefit and experience. I chose a top-tier institution because the academy is probably the most important marketplace of ideas on earth. It is the place where movers and shakers are made. It is important that the Christian faith and life be on display with all the other philosophies of our age, so that others may see the truth in it. Jennifer put it best, "Don't be afraid. Christ conquered all and academia is no exception."

Notes:

about the authors

Jeannette Webb

Jeannette has worked with high school students for over 25 years helping them develop public speaking, leadership, and interview skills, and prepare effective applications for scholarship competitions. As Oklahoma State University's first Truman Scholar, she went on to receive a B.S. in Human Development and an M.S. in Family Economics. She spent a decade with the OSU Cooperative Extension Service as 4-H and Youth Development Specialist and Resource Management Specialist before she became a home educator in 1993. She has been a homeschool support group leader, conference speaker, and trustee for the Oklahoma Christian Home Educator's Consociation. She currently writes the college admissions column for Practical Homeschooling magazine.

In 2005, Jeannette received the Presidential Scholar Distinguished Teacher Award from the U.S. Department of Education. That same year she founded Aiming Higher Consultants to meet the unique needs of Christian students with big dreams.

Austin Webb

Homeschooled since second grade, Austin Webb has helped blaze new trails for the homeschool community. While in high school, Austin was named the John M. Stalnaker Memorial Merit Scholar (top all-around National Merit Scholar in the nation in science and math) for 2005 and was selected as a Presidential Scholar. As a junior he attended the highly competitive Research Science Institute at MIT where he worked on a project in neurobiology which later achieved national semifinalist standing in both the Intel Science Talent Search and the Siemens Westinghouse competition. He was accepted to some of the world's best colleges including Harvard, MIT, Caltech, and the University of Chicago with offers of hundreds of thousands of dollars in scholarships.

He matriculated to the California Institute of Technology, graduating with honors in 2009 with a B.S. in theoretical computer science. In his spare time, he was involved in the Caltech Christian Fellowship and gourmet cooking competitions.

During his undergraduate career, Austin undertook multiple research projects including the topics of quantum computing, quantum chaos theory, and classifying the computational difficulty of a major economic equilibrium problem.

He was recently awarded a highly prestigious Graduate Research Fellowship from the National Science Foundation. Austin will receive an NSF annual stipend for three years to fund his Ph.D. research at the University of Washington in Seattle. He was also awarded a Wissner-Slivka First Year Fellowship from the university.

In graduate school, Austin plans to work in the application of probabilistic and statistical techniques to problems in computer science, focusing on either randomized algorithms or on machine learning and data mining.

As Field Representative for Aiming Higher Consultants, Austin provides his wealth of experience to students interested in the technical fields and keeps up with the pulse of Christian scholars at top universities across America.

Natalie Webb

Home educated her entire life, Natalie is an accomplished musician, a nationally ranked platform speaker, and Co-Founder of The International Debate Society - an online venue for teaching Lincoln-Douglas debate. While in high school, she was a successful fund-raiser for a local Pregnancy Care Center and is well known in her community for her leadership activities.

She was accepted into the most prestigious colleges in the country - Princeton, Harvard, Cornell, Penn, Carnegie Mellon, and Rice, as well as highly competitive programs like Penn's Jerome Fisher Program in Management and Technology. She was offered hundreds of thousands in scholarships.

As practical as her brother is theoretical, Natalie is pursuing a degree in Operations Research and Financial Engineering at Princeton University. Her freshman year, she was selected as 1 of 35 students for the competitive Humanities Sequence, a great books course known as the crown jewel of the Princeton experience. She was the only engineer in this grinding four class series, which covered the landmark achievements of the Western intellectual tradition from antiquity to the modern period. She is involved in the Princeton Evangelical Fellowship, was a founding member of a baroque chamber group, and loves discussing life's big questions with friends.

As a Field Representative for Aiming Higher Consultants, Natalie offers special insights for those students interested in pursing engineering, music, or liberal arts.

dear parent

You know the possibilities for your child are endless, but sometimes it feels like you are all alone.

Not any longer!

I created **Aiming Higher Consultants** for parents just like you. Finally, there is a resource to help parents wade through all the decisions of the high school years - what classes to take, what tests to prepare for, what colleges to consider. And sometimes a shoulder to cry on.

Let me tell you a little bit about what we do. **Aiming Higher Consultants** is a college consulting firm dedicated to helping Christian students with undergraduate admissions to great schools. Our goal is to empower families to confidently navigate the difficult college application process by providing as much or as little assistance as is needed. We can help families to:

- Develop a comprehensive plan to promote the holistic development of each student
- Find the best college fit
- Formulate a marketing strategy that showcases the student's unique strengths
- Provide guidance for the entire college application process
- Evaluate the college essay topics and give feedback throughout the writing process
- Provide oversight as you design school documents
- Strategize how to solicit the most helpful recommendation letters
- Hone interview skills
- Prepare a résumé for interviews and scholarship applications

If you'd like to learn more about what we have to offer, please visit us at www.aiminghigherconsultants.com.

Blessings,

Jeannette Webb

resources

"Getting Into a Top College" was originally published in *Practical Homeschooling*, September/October 2005.

"SAT Prep for First Grade?" was originally published in *Practical Homeschooling*, May/June 2007.

"How I Trained My Children to Be Leaders" is based on an article originally published in *Practical Homeschooling*, November/December 2007.

"The Gift of a Mentor" was originally published in *Practical Homeschooling*, November/December 2007.

"Parents as Mentors" was originally published in *Practical Homeschooling*, January/February 2008.

"Raising Gifted Children Right" was originally published in *Practical Homeschooling*, May/June 2008.

"Regaining Our Pioneer Spirit: Staying Home and Standing Out" was originally published in *Practical Homeschooling*, March/April 2006.

"The Freshman Year of High School: Keep it Real" was originally published in *Practical Homeschooling*, March/April 2008.

"The Sophomore Year of High School: Emerging Butterflies" was originally published in *Practical Homeschooling*, May/June 2008.

"The Critical Jr. Year" was originally published in *Practical Homeschooling*, September/October 2007.

"Senior Year: The Final Lap" was originally published in *Practical Homeschooling*, September/October 2008.

"Turbo-charge Your High School Academics" was originally published in *Practical Homeschooling*, January/February 2006.

"PSAT/SAT/ACT and National Merit" was originally published in *Practical Homeschooing*, July/August 2008.

"Test Savvy" was originally published in *Practical Homeschooling*, May/June 2006.

"Choosing the Best High School Activities" was originally published in *Practical Homeschooling*, November/December 2005.

"Building a College Résumé" was originally published in *Practical Homeschooling*, January/February 2009.

"How to Pick a College" was originally published in *Practical Homeschooling*, November/December 2008.

"Selling Colleges on You" was originally published in *Practical Homeschooling*, July/August 2006.

"The College Application" was originally published in *Practical Homeschooling*, March/April 2009.

"Your College Admissions Essay" was originally published in *Practical Homeschooling*, September/October 2006.

"Essays that Bring Home the Bacon" was originally published in *Practical Homeschooling*, July/August 2007.

"The Counselor Letter" was originally published in *Practical Homeschooling*, May/June 2009.

"Getting Great College Recommendations" was originally published in *Practical Homeschooling*, January/February 2007.

"College Interviews" was originally published in *Practical Homeschooling*, November/December 2006.

"How Dangerous is College?" is based on an article originally published in *Practical Homeschooling*, March/April 2007.

All articles used by permission. Copyright © 2010 Home Life, Inc.

CPSIA information can be obtained at www.ICGtesting.com
Printed in the USA
LVOW071519250412

279141LV00001B/93/P